Differentiated MATH

Tools & Activities to Get Students Moving, Thinking & Learning

by Donna VanderWeide, M.S.

Crystal Springs BOOKS

SDE

a division of Staff Development for Educators

Peterborough, New Hampshire

Published by Crystal Springs Books
A division of Staff Development for Educators (SDE)
10 Sharon Road, PO Box 500
Peterborough, NH 03458
1-800-321-0401
www.SDE.com/crystalsprings

Published 2008
Printed in the United States of America
12 11 10   2   3   4   5

ISBN: 978-1-884548-98-7

        Library of Congress Cataloging-in-Publication Data

VanderWeide, Donna, 1938-
   Differentiated math : tools & activities to get students moving, thinking & learning / by Donna VanderWeide.
        p. cm.
   ISBN 978-1-884548-98-7
1. Mathematics--Study and teaching (Elementary)--Activity programs. 2. Individualized instruction. I. Title.

   QA135.6.V376 2008
   372.7--dc22

                        2007034237

Acknowledgments

Vicki Alger is my desktop editor and the other half of my brain. Thank you, Vicki, for taking my global thoughts and organizing them for the rest of the world!

Thank you, too, to the Association for the Integration of Math and Science (AIMS) training staff, who through countless workshops and resource books have shaped my math thinking.

Editor: Sharon Smith
Art Director and Designer: S. Dunholter
Production Coordinator: Deborah Fredericks
Illustrators: Marci McAdam and Jill Shaffer

This book is dedicated to three women mathematicians who have influenced my thinking about how math should be taught in the elementary setting:

Mary Baratta-Lorton, author of *Mathematics Their Way*. Her approach to teaching math was a revelation and changed me forever.

Marilyn Burns, author of *About Teaching Mathematics*. Marilyn's view of math as a continuum of skills that reaches across grades K through 8 was an inspiration to me. Now I think beyond just my own grade level.

Kim Sutton, one of the original Association for the Integration of Math and Science (AIMS) trainers and the author of many math books for elementary teachers. I saw in Kim's many workshops the joy and flexibility of "finding it out for myself."

We often think of math as being a male-dominated field, so to these women I want to say, "Thank you!"

CONTENTS

INTRODUCTION

You know how to differentiate your instruction with language arts. You've learned how to "unbutton" your thinking to show your students how and why you do what you do when you read. You think out loud as you reason through a piece of literature. You move on to guided practice, which gives you a chance to listen in and give feedback on new and developing skills. Students go off to independent practice, and then they come back to the group to share what they have learned. Anchor charts, scribed by you, record the group thinking and understandings that emerge during sharing time. Light bulbs go on as the discussion goes deeper. Students build on each other's thinking and solidify their own understandings. Finally, they record their learning in their journals, so they can go back and see their reasoning and the problem-solving strategies they used.

Now, as the United States educational system becomes more and more standards based, we see new attention being paid to math. The logical question is: if differentiation works so well in language arts, will it work just as well in math? Sure it will! But how do you apply those ideas in math class? How can you differentiate when there are basic facts that build on each other as the student moves up the grades? How can you keep so many students from becoming "math phobic" at the fourth-grade level, when these basic facts and algorithms should be automatic?

Make It a Help, Not a Burden

Differentiating is not something you do every minute for every child in your class. It does not need to be overwhelming. Instead you can choose to differentiate *when it's appropriate* *and will increase learning*. Differentiation is a tool to be included in your instructional toolbox. Make it a benefit, not a burden!

Differentiated Math gives you the answers. The differentiated math class described in this book includes energizers and other whole-class activities. Its focus, however, is on math lab. Math lab is an opportunity for kids to practice and review in a hands-on way what has already been introduced in a more structured whole-group or small-group setting, and to share with each other their mathematical thinking.

Differentiated Math provides you with tools and activities for a wide range of learners and learning. Use the ideas included here to make assessments and plan activities for your students in whole-group, small-group, and individualized settings. Try the whole-class warm-ups (energizers), the individualized or paired explorations, the task cards, and the physical games. Introduce basic concepts and vocabulary early in the year with "Training Camp for Graphs and Glyphs" and use the other graph and glyph activities throughout the year to further develop skills and encourage mathematical thinking. Entice your young learners with the food activities. Reinforce their learning with all the opportunities to use mini math lab books (for short-term reference) and math journals (for a more permanent record of how student thinking evolves over time). You'll find lots of choices here to accommodate the learning needs of all your students, keep them interested, and help them to meet your state's standards.

Sound like fun? It is! And students whose teachers use the math lab approach will agree. Here's how to make it work for you and your students:

1. Identify the first unit with which you want to use differentiation.

2. Make a copy of the "Unit Lesson Plan Checklist" (pages 166–67) and use it as a tool to be sure you're differentiating your instruction.

3. Take advantage of the reproducibles on pages 73 and 175–78, or substitute your own tools, to pre-assess your students' learning styles, outside interests, multiple intelligences, and readiness.

4. Copy the Differentiated Daily Lesson Plan Template (page 170) and use it as a guide for deciding how to allocate your math time.

5. Try as many of the tools and strategies in this book as you can!

6. Continue your assessments on an ongoing basis.

7. At the end of the year, complete your post-assessments and, with your students, celebrate the learning that has taken place in your classroom this year!

Those are the basics. I would ask you to leave the workbooks on the shelf. Take another look at the standards you are asked to teach and at the Curriculum Focal Points established by the National Council of Teachers of Mathematics (NCTM), published in September 2006. You will be relieved to know that the newest approach recommended by NCTM is to stop teaching "a mile wide and an inch deep" and, instead, to focus on basics that build on each other each year from prekindergarten through eighth grade.

As you explore the strategies in this book, I think you'll be excited to see how much energy differentiation can add to your math class. This approach can help you put the "plus" back in math with games and hands-on activities and leave out the "minus" of repetitive drills with no real-world connections. When you look at the best times you've had teaching math, and the times your students' thinking developed the most, you will find the seeds for differentiation. Let's make those seeds grow!

ENERGIZERS

Energizers are quick whole-group activities that get students on their feet and moving with a purpose as they begin math time. They're especially good for kinesthetic and spatial learners. Energizers are preview and review games, songs, and rhymes that engage students and focus their attention. They're structured to encourage participation and build accountability on the part of every student, with an effort made to give everyone plenty of opportunities to ask and answer questions.

Energizers encourage strong collaboration and cooperation among students, building a sense of community in the classroom and laying the foundation for later work in small groups. Working together also builds higher-level thinking skills. When students share their thinking, they expand and enrich their thinking, achieving deeper understandings and making connections in ways they might never accomplish independently.

So what do energizers have to do with differentiation? In addition to engaging every child, they offer students a variety of different pathways to learning. Your auditory learners will love the way the songs in this chapter give them memory clues, such as using "Twinkle, Twinkle, Little Star" to help them spell "eight." Kinesthetic learners will respond to the opportunity to reinforce their learning with movement. And visual learners will find plenty of visual cues to help them, too. So you're reaching all learning styles without a lot of additional prep time for yourself. That's differentiation at its best.

Energizers are a good lead-in to math time in a practical sense, too. Because these activities can be completed pretty quickly, many of them (such as "Scramble Freeze Tag" and

"Match Mate") work well as a way to get kids into pairs or small groups for other activities. Some of the energizers make particularly good introductions to specific sets of task cards in the Math Lab Options chapter.

When you get to the songs on pages 28–44, I recommend that you photocopy them onto overheads or write the words out on chart paper for students to follow. Then sing each song together as a class. More detailed instructions for all of the other activities are included in the following pages. Feel free to incorporate movement ideas that you and your students generate together.

Now go ahead; get your students moving, talking, listening, and learning!

Corner to Corner

Procedure

Assign 1 "Corner to Corner" choice to each of the 4 corners of your room. Label each corner. While students remain seated, have each child pick 1 of the choices you've offered and write her choice on her paper. On your cue, each student goes to the corner she's chosen and finds a partner in that same corner. Partners then discuss their reasons for choosing as they did.

Examples of Corner to Corner Choices:

- Favorite math activity: addition, subtraction, graphing, or calendars
- What do you feel like today?: hummingbird, eagle, wren, or mockingbird

Extension

Label each corner with a different number. Have each student come up with an equation for which the answer is a number in 1 of the corners, then go to the appropriate corner and compare equations with another student who's created an equation for that same number. So if the number in 1 corner is 27, 1 child might have 9 x 3 and another might have 20 + 7.

What is your favorite math activity?
Addition
Subtraction
Graphing
Calendars

Sign Off

MATERIALS

FOR EACH STUDENT

- 1 copy of work sheet
- Pencil

Preparation

Create a "Sign Off" work sheet with a variety of math-related questions on it.

Procedure

Give each student a copy of the work sheet. Explain that each student is to circulate throughout the room, seeking out other students who can answer the questions on his sheet. Note that each student may answer no more than 1 question on any other student's sheet. When the "seeker" finds another student who can answer 1 of the questions on his sheet, he asks that person to fill in the answer and then sign her name next to it. The seeker and the signer must agree that the answer is correct. As soon as a student has a sheet on which all of the questions have been answered and signed, that student then sits down and becomes a resource person for other students who are stuck or who want to check an answer. Once all work sheets are completed, review the answers as a class.

Examples of Questions for Sign Off Work Sheet:

- Count by 2s to 20
- Name a geometric shape
- Name a coin value
- Measure an item
- Identify a fractional part that is shaded
- Extend a number pattern (2, 4, 6, . . .)

Match Mate

MATERIALS

FOR EACH STUDENT

- 1 card

Preparation

Make up pairs of "Match Mate" cards. (If you have an odd number of students, allow for 1 trio.)

Procedure

Give 1 card to each student. Students move about the room, exchanging cards as they pass each other. After a few minutes, call, "Freeze!" Students stop switching cards. When you call, "Match Mate," each student looks for the other student who has a card that matches his. As each match pairs off, they stop and hold their cards in the air. When all students have found their matches, begin again.

Examples of Pairs for Match Mate:

- Numerals and number words
- Dot patterns and numerals
- Problems and solutions
- Money and values
- Fractions and equivalent fractions

Fact or Fib

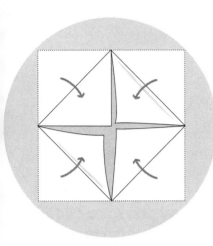

MATERIALS

FOR EACH STUDENT
- 1 piece of paper, cut to 8 1/2 x 8 1/2 inches
- Pencil

FOR THE TEACHER
- 1 piece of paper, cut to 8 1/2 x 8 1/2 inches
- Pencil

Procedure

Give each student a square of paper. Demonstrate folding the paper diagonally from corner to corner as students follow your lead. Unfold and repeat with the other corners. Unfold again and show students that now the folds form an "x" across the paper. Model folding each corner up to the center of the "x." Everyone should now have 4 triangular flaps with points meeting at the center of the paper.

Next, each student writes 1 statement on the outside of each of his 4 flaps. All 4 statements should be believable, but only 3 should be true. The fourth statement should be an almost true fib. On the inside of that flap, the student needs to indicate that this one is the fib.

Now give students 5 minutes to walk around and present their "Fact or Fib" papers to each other. Student 1 presents her "Fact or Fib" sheet to Student 2. Student 2 must guess which statement is the fib. If Student 2 correctly guesses which statement is the fib, Student 1 moves on to another student. If Student 2 incorrectly guesses which statement is the fib, then Student 2 must sign his name on the inside of Student 1's folded sheet. The student with the most signatures is the winner.

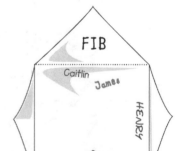

Examples of Subjects for Fact or Fib:
- Problems and answers
- Next in a pattern
- Numbers greater than, less than, or equal to other numbers or equations (An example of a fact would be "16 < 25." A fib would be "18 + 8 = 27.")

What's My Line?

Procedure

Ask a question that relates to the students themselves and for which different students will have different answers. You might ask "What is your birthday?" Designate 1 corner of the room as 1 end of a continuum and the opposite corner of the room as the other end of the continuum. For example, if birthdays are the topic, then identify 1 corner of the room as January 1 and the other corner as December 31.

Instruct students to align themselves physically along the continuum based on their answers. Explain that this must be done **without talking.** This encourages students to use body language, nonverbal communication, facial expressions, appropriate touching, and other bodily-kinesthetic clues as they align themselves.

Examples of Ordering Questions for What's My Line?:

• Birthdays: from January 1 to December 31

• Height: from the shortest child to the tallest child (or vice versa)

Variations

1. Give each child a card with a whole number, fraction, or picture of some currency combination. Based on these cards, have students put themselves in order from lowest to highest, smallest to largest, or least to greatest.

2. Give each child a length of string and have them arrange themselves from shortest piece to longest.

January 1	December 31

Percentage What's My Line?

MATERIALS

- 10 index cards
- Marker

Preparation

Mark each index card with a percentage; start with 10 percent and continue in 10 percent increments through 100 percent. Establish a continuum along 1 wall of the classroom by posting the index cards in order along the wall at a point above the height of the students.

Procedure

Explain that each student is to predict the results of an upcoming class survey by standing under the percent card that corresponds to her prediction. Encourage students to discuss why each chose to stand in a particular place.

Examples of Questions for Percentage What's My Line?:

- What percentage of the class will see the newest upcoming film?
- What percentage of the class will read the newest book?

Place My Face

MATERIALS

FOR EACH STUDENT
- 1 large card

Preparation

Prepare cards with pictures or numbers related to the topic you're studying.

Procedure

Tape 1 card to each student's back. Explain that there's **no looking!** Students walk around the room. When you say, "Place the face," students pair up and look at the cards on each other's backs. One student in each pair asks her partner 3 yes or no questions ("Am I greater than 5?"), then guesses what's on her card. If she's correct, her partner removes the card and places it on the student's front. Then the partners trade roles and repeat the process. Once a student's card is on her front and she's finished answering her partner's questions, she becomes a helper to anyone who still has a card on his back and the questioning continues.

Examples for Place My Face Cards:

- Numbers from 1 through 50
- Geometric shapes
- Amounts of money
- Operations (+, −, x, ÷)

Scramble Freeze Tag WHOLE GROUP

Procedure

When you say, "Scramble," students begin to move around the classroom. They continue until you say, "Freeze!" At that point, students get ready to form a group with those who happen to be standing nearby. They must form a group of a certain size, and that size depends on the answer to a question you ask (for example, "How many digits in '306'?"). Once you ask your question, students silently determine the number. When you say, "Tag," students form groups of that number (in this case, 3). "Leftovers" form a group at the front of the room until the next Scramble is announced; then they rejoin the whole group.

Examples of Cues for Scramble Freeze Tag:

- Number of times you clap
- Answer to an addition or subtraction problem
- Number placement ("the number in the tens place in 527")
- Number of cups in a quart

Your Number's Up  4–6 STUDENTS

MATERIALS

FOR EACH GROUP
- 1 die
- 1 copy of the reproducible directions (page 19)

Procedure

Introduce "Probability Cubes Games" (pages 72–77) with this energizer, which builds instant recognition of dot patterns and addition facts.

Divide students into groups. Distribute all the materials and let groups proceed on their own.

 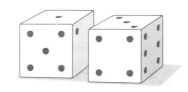 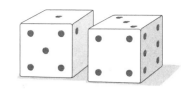

STUDENT DIRECTIONS
FOR YOUR NUMBER'S UP

- Stay with your group.

- The goal is for your group to roll a total of 56 or more before any other group.

- Each member of the group should take a turn rolling 1 die.

- When you roll a number, you must complete the activity for that number before passing the die to the next person.

- Every student is a recorder. You need to keep a running total of where your team stands.

Rules for Rollers

- Roll a 1: Recite your name, birthday, and favorite food before passing the die to the next roller.

- Roll a 2: Good roll! Pass the die on.

- Roll a 3: Get up, run around the circle, and sit down before passing the die to the next roller.

- Roll a 4: Good roll! Pass the die on.

- Roll a 5: Sing the first line of "Row, Row, Row Your Boat."

- Roll a 6: Start over. All previous scores are erased.

I Have/Who Has

Inexpensive paper plates are the ideal way to "serve up" review and practice for those 5 minutes before lunch or dismissal. Because this activity gets kids up and moving, it's a great brain break as well as a good way to practice those rote-learning tasks.

I have
7.
Who has
10+5?

I have
15.
Who has
12−4?

MATERIALS

- 10 to 30 lightweight 9-inch paper plates
- Red and blue markers

Game Preparation

1   Decide how many plates you want to use. Students can help each other, so you don't have to have a plate for every child. On the other hand, if you have more plates than students, someone can have more than 1 plate.

2   Write an "I have" statement at the top of the first plate with a red permanent marker. For example, you might write, "I have 7."

3   Under that statement, use a blue permanent marker to write a "Who has?" question. This could be something like "Who has 8 + 2?"

4   On the next plate, write the answer to the question on the first plate (in this case, "I have 10."). Under that write a new question ("Who has 5 − 3?").

5   Continue writing answers and questions on plates until you get to the last plate. Make sure that last question is answered on the first plate! (Some people call this "Zip Around" because the answer always ends up back where the game began—with the first plate.)

6   Laminate all the plates so that you can play this game again and again.

To Play

1   Pass out the plates to the students.

2   You play this game just as you'd play "Popcorn." Ask any student to begin the game by standing and reading his plate, then quickly sitting down. Note on the chalkboard the time you start.

3   Whoever has the answer to the first student's question is next to stand. He reads the answer and the question on his plate, then sits down.

4   The game continues until it comes back to the student who went first. He stands, reads the answer on his plate, and sits down.

5   After the first run through, tell students how long it took them to get through all the plates. Ask them if they think they can "beat the clock" when they do it again. Usually students will respond with a great roar of "Yes!"

6   Have students trade plates and go again. If you have fewer plates than students, ask some students to give their plates to others who haven't had turns.

Examples

Plate 1: I have 2 + 2. Who has the number after 6?

Plate 2: I have 7. Who has 6 – 3?

Plate 1: I have 3:00. Who has the hour hand on 4 and the minute hand on 6?

Plate 2: I have 4:30. Who has the hour hand on 5 and the minute hand on 12?

Variation

If you prefer, start with the reproducibles on the following pages. Copy both pages, cut the boxes apart, and then glue 1 box onto each paper plate.

I HAVE/WHO HAS

NURSERY RHYME NUMBERS

Copy, cut apart, and glue each block onto a paper plate.

I have the number of fingers on both hands. **Who has** the number of men in TWO tubs?	**I have** one, two. **Who has** the number of the days of Christmas?
I have six. **Who has** the time in "Hickory Dickory Dock"?	**I have** 12. **Who has** the numbers for shut the door?
I have 1:00. **Who has** the number of wives going to St. Ives?	**I have** three, four. **Who has** the number of days in September?
I have seven. **Who has** the time for the scholar?	**I have** 30 days. **Who has** the number for pick up sticks?
I have 10:00. **Who has** the numbers for buckle my shoe?	**I have** five, six. **Who has** the ant who stopped to suck his thumb?

I HAVE/WHO HAS

NURSERY RHYME NUMBERS

(continued)

I have one. **Who has** the number of bags of wool for the black sheep?	**I have** 31. **Who has** the number of pigs who went to market?
I have three. **Who has** the number of wheels on the bus?	**I have** five. **Who has** the number of people who went up the hill?
I have four. **Who has** the number of days in February?	**I have** two. **Who has** the number of legs on Miss Muffet's spider?
I have 28. **Who has** the number of kittens plus their mittens?	**I have** eight. **Who has** the number of sheep that Little Bo Peep found?
I have 9. **Who has** the number of days in March?	**I have** zero. **Who has** ten?

My Poem, Your Poem, Our Poem!

MATERIALS

FOR EACH GROUP

- 2 copies of the reproducible (page 25)

Procedure

Introduce Math & Poetry task cards (pages 108–10) with this energizer, which helps to stimulate creativity, reinforce math concepts, and build communication skills. Divide students into groups, hand out the reproducibles, and review the instructions with students. Then turn them loose! After everyone's finished, be sure to share results as a class.

Geometry Rhyme & Rhythm

WHOLE GROUP

MATERIALS

- 1 overhead transparency of the "Shapes All Around" reproducible (page 26)
- 1 overhead transparency of the "Rap Around the Shapes" reproducible (page 27)

Procedure

Display the transparency of the "Shapes All Around" song on your overhead projector. As you sing the song together, have students find and point to examples of each shape. After each verse, ask each of several students to describe her shape and where she found it.

You can use the rap in a very similar way. As you recite it (with rhythm!), have students point to any examples of each shape or concept (such as symmetry) they can find in the room. When the rap stops, ask each of several students to describe his example and where he found it.

STUDENT DIRECTIONS FOR
MY POEM, YOUR POEM, OUR POEM!

1. As a group, write a number in each box in the poem.
2. Go back and read the poem you've made.
3. Solve the problem and explain your reasoning at the bottom of the page.
4. Prepare the poem for another group. On your second copy of this work sheet, fill in the boxes with the same numbers, but don't solve the problem!
5. Trade poems with another group.
6. Solve that group's poem problem while they solve yours.
7. Compare your answers with the other group's answers.

There were _____ ducks swimming on a lake so blue,

While high overhead _____ dozen geese flew.

They were all headed south in an orderly way,

Passing _____ swans who had little to say.

Near the water's edge, a flamingo stood tall,

As _____ pelicans and _____ dozen egrets had a ball.

They all frolicked and romped while searching for dinner,

But a new bird appeared, and it was the winner.

The prize was a fish that looked juicy and plump.

They could not believe it, those _____ frogs on the stump.

All the animals were looking for something to eat,

But it was the noisy seagull who became the animal to beat.

In this poem there were _____ animals mentioned.
This is our reasoning: _____

_____

SHAPES ALL AROUND
Tune: "The Farmer in the Dell"

Can you find the circles? Can you find the circles?
Can you find the circles going round, round, round?
Look for the circles. Look for the circles.
How many circles have you found, found, found?

Look for the triangles. Look for the triangles.
Look for the triangles. Count 1, 2, 3.
Look for the triangles. Look for the triangles.
How many triangles do you see?

Look for a rectangle. Look for a rectangle.
Look for the sides. Count 1, 2, 3, 4.
Look for a rectangle. Look for a rectangle.
It has 4 sides and no more, more, more.

Look for a square. Look for a square.
It's a special rectangle with sides the same.
Look for a square. Look for a square.
Say aloud with me, "The sides are all the same."

RAP AROUND THE SHAPES

Geometry, geometry; it's fun for me and you.
Listen carefully for all the fun things we can do.

Polygons, polygons all around.
Shapes everywhere can be found.

Triangles, circles, and squares, to name a few,
Pentagons, rectangles, and hexagons, too.

Cubes, spheres, and pyramids take up space.
Solid figures are seen in every place.

Geometry, geometry; it's fun for me and you.
Listen carefully for all the fun things we can do.

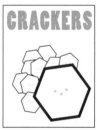

Put some shapes together and find the symmetry.
Then try some equal slices, so fractions you will see.

Large shapes, small shapes; some can be congruent.
Shaping up like this, there's really nothing to it.

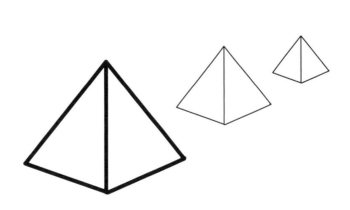

MONEY SONGS
Tune: "Are You Sleeping?"

The Penny

See the shiny penny, (2x)
Brown as it can be, (2x)
Showing Abe Lincoln, (2x)
For all of us to see. (2x)

He has a bushy beard (2x)
And a tall black hat. (2x)
A penny's worth 1 cent. (2x)
What do you think of that? (2x)

The Nickel

Thomas Jefferson (2x)
Will be found (2x)
On a nickel, (2x)
Silvery smooth and round. (2x)
It's smaller than a quarter (2x)
But bigger than a penny. (2x)
A nickel's worth 5 cents. (2x)
Have you any? (2x)

MONEY SONGS
Tune: "Are You Sleeping?"

The Dime
President Roosevelt (2x)
Sits on our dime. (2x)
The dime's our smallest coin. (2x)
We use it all the time. (2x)

It takes 2 nickels (2x)
To make up a dime. (2x)
Or count out 10 pennies (2x)
To finish this rhyme. (2x)

The Quarter
The father of our country, (2x)
George Washington, (2x)
Is stamped on our quarter. (2x)
Now isn't this fun? (2x)

It takes 5 nickels (2x)
Or 25 cents (2x)
To equal 1 quarter. (2x)
You knew what I meant. (2x)

SKIP COUNTING BY 5s
Tune: "Twinkle, Twinkle, Little Star"

5, 10, 15,
20, 25,
30, 35, 40, 45,
50, 55,
60, 65,
70, 75,
80, 85,
90, 95,
100.
We can count by 5s each time.

SKIP COUNTING BY 2s
Tune: "Three Blind Mice"

2, 4, 6,
8, 10, 12,
14, 16, 18,
20—all done.
Counting by 2s is easy, you see.
All you must do is keep up with me.
Now every kid can fast count with me
When I count by 2s.

SKIP COUNTING BY 10s
Tune: "Ten Little Indians"

10, 20, 30, 40, 50,
60, 70, 80, 90, 100.
Clap along as we count fast.
This little song just will not last.

DOUBLES & NEAR DOUBLES
Tune: "Oh My Darling Clementine"

When the same numbers are
  added together,
They are easy to repeat.
So get ready to start adding,
And then just keep up the
  beat.

2 and 2 equal 4.
3 and 3 are always 6.
4 and 4 equal 8.
5 and 5 are always 10.

6 and 6 equal 12.
7 and 7 are always 14.
8 and 8 equal 16.
9 and 9 equal 18.

Now here's a trick that you
  can do,
And I will do it, too.
When you get close to a
  double, I will add up with
  you.

2 and 3 now is 1 more
Than the double 2 and 2,
So it equals 5, not 4.
Near doubles help us
  through.

3 plus 4 is close to 6.
You remember how it's done.
Add 1 more and you get 7.
Near doubles are so much
  fun.

Now it's your turn to go
  adding;
Try it with 7 and 8.
Think of doubles and add 1
  more,
And you'll soon be doing
  great!

Now try 8 added to 9.
It's the best of adding time.
It's not 16 'cause it's 1 more.
You are doing really fine.

ZERO IS A HERO
Chant to: "Peanut, Peanut Butter & Jelly"

Ze-ro . . . is a hero! Yes!
Ze-ro . . . is a hero! Yes!
When you add or subtract, it happens every time.
Zero saves the number. Just write it on the line!
Ze-ro . . . is a hero! Yes!
Ze-ro . . . is a hero! Yes!

HOW MUCH IS A MILLION?
Tune: "She'll Be Coming 'Round the Mountain"

How much is a million? Do you know?
How much is a million? Do you know?
Take a 1 and then 6 zeros.
Take a 1 and then 6 zeros.
That's a lot of anything, don't you know!

MUSICAL NUMBER WORDS

ONE
Tune: "Three Blind Mice"

O-N-E, O-N-E,
Spells one for me,
Spells one for me.
I have 1 mouth, 1 nose, 1 head.
Just 1 little chair and 1 little bed.
Just O-N-E is what I said,
And that spells one—
O-N-E.

TWO
Tune: "She'll Be Coming 'Round the Mountain"

Can you think of all the things that come in 2s? 2! 2!
Can you think of all the things that come in 2s? 2! 2!
There are ears, hands, and eyes,
If you really want to try,
Just spell it T-W-O.
That says two.

Can you think of all the things that come in 2s? 2! 2!
Can you think of all the things that come in 2s? 2! 2!
You have arms and legs and feet—
You don't have to repeat.
It's just T-W-O
To spell two.

MUSICAL NUMBER WORDS

THREE
Tune: "Happy Birthday"

T-H-R-E-E,
Now what comes in 3s?
My tricycle, a triangle,
They all come in 3s.

T-H-R-E-E,
That surely spells three.
My mommy and daddy and me
Comes to 3.

FOUR
Tune: "Daisy"

F-O-U-R
That's how you spell four.
Dogs' legs, cats' legs—just 4 and no more.
The wheels around my wagon,
The tires my car can go on.
F-O-U-R
Let's square it up.
Just count with me up to 4.

MUSICAL NUMBER WORDS

FIVE
Tune: "Ten Little Indians"

F-I-V-E that spells five,
F-I-V-E that spells five,
F-I-V-E that spells five,
Like the fingers on 1 hand.

F-I-V-E that spells five,
F-I-V-E that spells five,
F-I-V-E that spells five,
Toes that wiggle on my foot.

SIX
Tune: "Shortenin' Bread"

S-I-X, that spells six.
Count this out and lay out sticks.
My dominoes and little dump truck
Need 6 parts to make them go.
S-I-X for little bee legs.
S-I-X for buzzing flies.
S-I-X that spells six.
S-I-X, that's 3 and 3.

MUSICAL NUMBER WORDS

SEVEN
Tune: "Pop Goes the Weasel"

S . . . -E-V-E-N,
Spell it out for 7.
S . . . -E-V-E-N,
Perfect stars in heaven.

EIGHT
Tune: "Twinkle, Twinkle, Little Star"

E-I-G-H-T,
4 and 4 this means for me.
8-legged spider in a spin.
2 little ponies race to win.
E-I-G-H-T,
4 and 4 this means to me.

NINE
Tune: "The Itsy Bitsy Spider"

N-I-N-E, that spells nine.
N-I-N-E, count this rhyme.
If you use your fingers,
If you use your toes,
Counting up to 9 will leave you
With 1 more.

MUSICAL NUMBER WORDS

TEN

Tune: "Camptown Races"

1, 2, 3, and 4 and 5,
Count it! Count it!
6 and 7, 8, 9, 10,
T-E-N spells ten.
Hold up both your feet,
Both your hands as well.
T-E-N counts every toe,
Like bouncing with your ball.

(On the last line, take a ball and bounce it.)

SWING & SWAY THE MONTHS AWAY

SEPTEMBER TOM-TOM
Tune: "Ten Little Indians"

S-e-p-t-e-m-b-e-r,
S-e-p-t-e-m-b-e-r,
S-e-p-t-e-m-b-e-r,
First month of the fall.

Making new friends, greeting old ones;
Trying new things, thinking new thoughts.
I'm so glad to use my big brain,
Right here in my brand-new room.

Leaves are changing to bright colors.
Daylight time is getting shorter.
Football fans are shouting louder.
We love games this time of year.

OCTOBER CHILLIES
Tune: "Teddy Bear Picnic"

O-c-t-o-b-e-r, the scariest month of all.
O-c-t-o-b-e-r, you'd better stay where you are.
For flying things go bump in the night,
And children will say with all of their might,
They'll have the scariest costumes in sight
To trick-or-treat to.

SWING & SWAY THE MONTHS AWAY

NOVEMBER MUNCHIES
Tune: "This Old Man"

N-o-v-
e-m-b-
e-r is November.
Turkey, sauce, and pumpkin pie—
It's eating time, and we know why.

Thank you here, thank you there—
Every family wants to share
Time together; it's a real treat,
Especially when we get to eat.

DECEMBER CELEBRATIONS
Tune: "Up on the Housetop"

D-e-c-e-m-b-e-r
Spells December, near and far.
Dress up in red and green and white,
With decorated trees it's quite a sight!

Gifts are wrapped and cookies baked.
Lights are hung and carols sung.
Is there a happier time to sing
And listen to the bells that like to ring?

SWING & SWAY THE MONTHS AWAY

JANUARY SHIVERS
Tune: "Let It Snow"

Oh, the month is January,
And the weather is contrary.
Let's try to spell it out,
J-a-n-u-a-r and then y.

We've got our coats and gloves
And the warmest hats we found.
But sledding and skating's best
When we sit by the fire and rest.

FEBRUARY LOVES
Tune: "The Muffin Man"

F-e-b-r-u-a-r-y.
F-e-b-r-u-a-r-y.
F-e-b-r-u-a-r-y.
The sweetest month of all.

28 days most of the time,
28 days most of the time,
28 days most of the time—
Leap year adds 1 more.

MARCH ALONG
Tune: "The Ants Go Marching"

March comes on like a lion's pounce—
M-a-r, c-h.
March comes on like a lion's pounce—
M-a-r, c-h.
The weather changes from warm to cold.
It's lion then lamb, so I've been told.
So I switch from coat to shirt,
And there's ice, then mud, then dirt.
Squash, slip, slide.

Hot, then warm, then very cold—
It's March, you see.
The weather is changing 3 times a day.
That's March, they say.
Well, I'm ready for it to be this or that,
And put away my winter hat.
So let the weather be—
Not hot, not cold, just right for me!

SWING & SWAY THE MONTHS AWAY

APRIL SHOWERS

Tune: "I'm Forever Blowing Bubbles"

I'm forever dodging raindrops—
Raindrops falling through the air.
Clouds seem to cry
As they go by.
April's the month
I can't stay dry.
A-p-r-i-l
Wettest month I see.
It's forever raining on me.
But soon flowers I will see.

MAY MELODY

Tune: "Skip to My Lou"

Mother's Day in M-a-y,
Mother's Day in M-a-y,
Mother's Day in M-a-y,
Love my mother every day.

To our classmates we must say,
School will end soon, now it's May.
We had fun and learned things, too.
There was just so much to do.

SWING & SWAY THE MONTHS AWAY

JUNE TUNE
Tune: "Daisy"

J-u-n-e—
It's the best month of all.
Sunny outside—
Let's go toss a ball.
Summer soon will be here.
School has gone for this year.
It's time to play, every day,
Till school begins again.

JULY JIVE
Tune: "When the Saints Go Marching In"

J-u-l-y.
J-u-l-y.
It's time to celebrate.
So come on and see the fireworks,
'Cause it's summer and it's great!

J-u-l-y.
J-u-l-y.
Come, let's take off to the beach.
Let's spread the blanket for a picnic
And keep the ants beyond our reach.

SWING & SWAY THE MONTHS AWAY

AUGUST CALLS
Tune: "Twinkle, Twinkle, Little Star"

Can you hear the school bell ring?
It can mean 1 special thing.
Summer's over;
Fall is near.
It's a special time of year.
A-U-G-U-S-T
Back to school for you and me.

MONTHS OF THE YEAR
Tune: "The Macarena"

January, February, March, April,
May, June, July, August,
September, October, November,
December.
Twelve months of the year.

(ADD THE ACTIONS OF "THE MACARENA" TO
YOUR WORDS.)

MATH EXPLORATIONS

Anytime you are going to be presenting new material, give your students the opportunity to freely explore the properties of the math tools they're about to use before they begin to work in a more structured setting. Students need time to work with each tool on their own—time for counting, measuring, describing, patterning, classifying, organizing, and communicating their reasoning. At the same time, you as a teacher need opportunities to assess each student's ability to apply specific mathematical concepts and communication skills. Explorations offer a chance for all those things.

In this section, you and your students benefit from open-ended explorations of materials that encourage different levels of thinking. The following activities are similar to energizers but are more individualized, offering opportunities for children to take charge of their own learning. With energizers, the teacher is running the show; with explorations, children determine how they will learn.

These are hands-on, "brains-on" activities that can be used for pre-assessment. Once you've used them to assess each child's readiness, you can plan where in the instruction cycle that child needs to begin.

Open–Ended Math Exploration

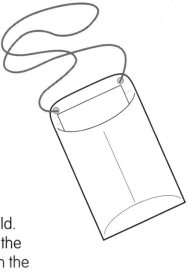

This is a good way to help students internalize the properties of numbers and of fact families. As students progress, be sure to change their target cards so students are appropriately challenged. This approach allows you to differentiate by updating individual cards as needed.

MATERIALS

FOR THE TEACHER
- Hole punch

FOR EACH CHILD
- Library pocket
- 18-inch length of yarn
- Number card or math flash card
- Mini math lab book (see pages 181–83)

FOR THE CLASS
- Tubs of manipulatives (Unifix cubes, buttons, number cubes, number links, teddy bear counters, or assorted small toys)

Preparation

1   Before class, create a library-pocket "necklace" for each child. Punch 2 holes near the top of the pocket, string the yarn through the holes, and tie the yarn ends together.

2   In each child's library pocket, insert a target card—a number card or flash card that shows a number or fact family the child needs to learn.

Procedure

1   If students have not previously had a chance to work with the materials in the tubs, allow 1 period for them just to "mess" with the materials. Students need this time to acquaint themselves with the possibilities of the manipulatives; once they've done this, they will be ready to listen to your specific instructions regarding ways to use the materials. This free-exploration time also gives you a chance to watch what different students do with the materials and to listen in on their conversations. The insights you gain from these on-the-spot assessments will inform your instruction.

2   Take time at the beginning of 1 or 2 work periods to model how to use the cards in the library pockets in conjunction with the tubs of materials. Let's say you give yourself a card with the number 7. Demonstrate how you would take similar objects (all buttons or all Unifix cubes) from the tubs and count out 7.

3   Divide students into groups of 4 to 6. This gives you a chance to move among the groups and give feedback as needed.

4   Hand out the library-pocket necklaces and tubs of materials. Give students a chance to practice counting the appropriate numbers of manipulatives on their own.

5   The next day, again model how to count the materials. Then take a mini math lab book and demonstrate how students are to record their findings. Show how they can use pictures or numbers to record what they've found. Still assuming that the number in your necklace is 7, you might draw a picture of 7 buttons.

6   Again divide students into groups of 4 to 6 and hand out the necklaces and the tubs of materials. This time, make sure each student has a mini math lab book as well.

7   Ask each student to count out the materials she chooses to represent what's on her card.

8   Explain that each student should then record what she's done—following your model—in her mini math lab book.

9   Ask students to share their books with the rest of their group or with the whole class.

Potato Investigations

Here's a hands-on way to teach sorting, counting, and patterning. This can also be done with other foods, such as pears, lemons, or apples.

MATERIALS

- Real potatoes of various sizes, colors, and types—at least 1 per student

Procedure

1   Teach students this counting-on chant: 1 potato, 2 potato, 3 potato, 4. 5 potato, 6 potato, 7 potato, more.

2   Have students play the traditional game that goes with the chant.

3   Give children a chance to work in small groups to sort, count, and pattern the potatoes.

4   Give students some examples of vocabulary words that describe comparative sizes ("smaller," "smallest," and so on).

5   Give each student 1 of the potatoes. Ask what each student notices about his potato. "I have a large, knobby potato." "I have a small potato that has very few bumps."

6   See if the group can find 2 potatoes that are alike in some way. Make a set of 2.

7   Repeat with 3 potatoes and then 4 potatoes.

8   Choose a large potato and a small potato and begin an A-B pattern (large-small). Ask students to read the pattern with you. Ask who's holding a potato that would come next in the pattern and have that student add her potato. Repeat and extend the pattern.

Button Explorations

Because buttons come with a variety of attributes (shapes and colors are just the beginning), they are ideal for explorations that involve sorting and classifying. Ask parents to send in any extra buttons they may have. You can also get buttons from crafts stores, catalogs, and Internet sites such as www. orientaltrading.com.

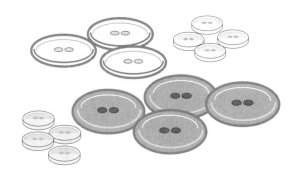

MATERIALS

FOR EACH STUDENT
- 1 small sorting tray

FOR THE CLASS
- Buttons, buttons, and more buttons!
- Clear plastic tennis ball containers for storing the buttons

Procedure

1   Distribute the buttons to the students.

2   Lead the students in singing "Buttons Everywhere" (see box) together all the way through, looking at their collections of buttons while they sing.

3   Sing the song together again. This time, after singing each verse together, have students look for buttons with the attributes described in that verse.

4   Pair off students. One student in each pair determines the categories he wants to use and groups his button collection into those categories. Then the partner must guess the sorting rule.

Buttons Everywhere

Tune: "Ten Little Indians"

Buttons, buttons, who's got buttons?
Buttons, buttons, who's got buttons?
Buttons, buttons, who's got buttons?
Right here in your hand.

Red and white and yellow buttons,
White and black and brown buttons,
Orange, green, and purple buttons,
Right here in your hand.

Some with 2 holes; some with 3 holes.
Some with 4 holes; some with no holes.
Some are round and some are square,
Right here in your hand.

Some are plastic; some are metal.
Some have pictures; some have flowers.
Some are leather; some are fabric,
Right here in your hand.

Investigations with Raisins

You can gain real insight into student understandings as you watch children work with "guesstimation" (making an estimate without a frame of reference) and then "estimation" (working with a frame of reference to make an informed decision). "Investigations with Raisins" also reveals a great deal about students' abilities to use "mental math" as well as their understanding of the terms "median," "mode," and "range." Most important, you will learn a lot as you watch students organize their data.

Note: Be sure to allow plenty of time. It can take as much as 45 minutes to complete all stages of this activity and the extension that follows.

MATERIALS

FOR THE CLASS

- 1 transparency of "Directions for Investigations with Raisins" reproducible (page 52)

FOR EACH STUDENT

- A 1/2-ounce box of raisins
- 1 clean paper plate
- 2 x 1 1/2-inch sticky notes
- 1 mini math lab book (see pages 181–83)

FOR THE TEACHER

- Chart paper
- Marker

Procedure

1   Divide students into groups of 4 to 6.

2   Place the transparency on the overhead. (This keeps students on task and helps avoid misunderstandings.)

3   Hand out the boxes of raisins, the paper plates, and the sticky notes.

4   Make sure each student has a mini math lab book.

5   Read the directions on the overhead with students. Keep the transparency in place so that they can refer back to it.

6   As students work, take the opportunity to "clipboard cruise" (walk around the room with a clipboard) and informally assess each student's problem-solving strategy.

7   Copy the Raisin Counts Chart (see illustration) onto a sheet of chart paper. Make sure each of the blocks on the chart is large enough to hold 1 sticky note.

8   When everyone has counted raisins, it's time to begin working with the chart. As you call out 1 range of numbers at a time, ask who has a count that falls within that range. Each of those students should add his sticky note in the appropriate column, beginning at the bottom. The sticky notes will form a graph.

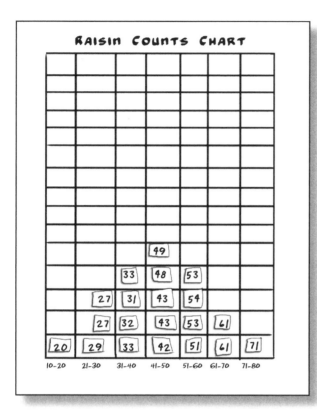

9 This is your chance to point out median (the value in the middle), mode (the value that appears the most), and range (the difference between the least and greatest values).

10 Have students follow the remaining directions to complete the activity.

Extended Raisin Investigations

4-6 STUDENTS

Once students have completed the basic raisin investigations, use this activity to promote more advanced thinking and reasoning.

MATERIALS

FOR EACH GROUP
1 box (1 1/2 ounces) raisins
1 copy of the "Directions for Extended Raisin Investigations" reproducible (page 53)

Procedure

1 Divide students into groups of 4 to 6.

2 Hand out the raisins and reproducibles.

3 Ask each group to follow the directions on the reproducible.

DIRECTIONS FOR
INVESTIGATIONS WITH RAISINS

1. Each person will need:
   - A 1/2-ounce box of raisins
   - Paper plate
   - Sticky notes and pencil
   - Mini math lab book

2. Look at your box of raisins and guess how many raisins are in the box.

3. Write your guesstimate at the top of a sticky note.

4. Open your box and count the raisins that are visible on the very top. Leave the raisins in the box!

5. Estimate how many raisins are in your entire box based on this frame of reference. Write that estimate on the bottom of the sticky note.

6. Empty your box and arrange the raisins on your plate. Count the raisins.

7. Write on a new sticky note the number of raisins you have.

8. Have your new sticky note with your raisin count ready to add to the class chart.

9. Look at everyone's numbers on the graph and predict with your small group how many raisins are usually in a box.

10. In your mini math lab book write:
    - What I have learned about guesstimate and estimate
    - My definition of median, mode, and range

DIRECTIONS FOR EXTENDED RAISIN INVESTIGATIONS

1. As a group, estimate the number of raisins contained in your 1 1/2-ounce box. Explain your reasoning in writing on the back of this sheet. Be ready to report to the whole class.

2. Count the raisins in the box. Figure out a way to share them equally.

3. Answer these questions:

- How many raisins were in your group's box? _____

- How did you count them? _____
  _____

- How did you share the raisins evenly? (Write out your reasoning.)
  _____
  _____

- Did you have any problem getting the raisins to come out evenly?
  _____

- If you did, how did you solve the problem?
  _____

- Was this fair to everyone?
  _____

- How else could you have divided the raisins to make it a fair share?
  _____

Paired Possibilities

This is an activity the whole class can complete at the same time, working in pairs. It's a good way to reinforce logical thinking.

MATERIALS

FOR EACH PAIR

- 1 piece of 8 1/2 x 11-inch paper
- Scissors
- Pencils
- Scratch paper

Procedure

1   Pair off students and give each pair 1 piece of paper.

2   Have each pair fold the paper into 8 equal sections.

3   Have them unfold the paper, cut the sections apart, and divide the pieces of paper evenly so that each student gets 4 pieces of paper.

4   Introduce the next step by saying, "You have grown so quickly over the last 6 months that all your clothes are too small for you. Your mother takes you shopping and buys you 3 shirts, 3 pairs of pants, and 2 pairs of shoes. I want you to figure out: by wearing these clothes in different combinations, how many different outfits could you make with your new clothes?"

5   Have students draw their new shirts, pants, and shoes, putting 1 picture on each section of paper. One student draws 3 pairs of pants and 1 pair of shoes—each picture on a different section of paper. The other student draws 3 shirts and 1 pair of shoes—again with each picture on a different section of paper.

6   Encourage pairs to manipulate their pictures to make different combinations of outfits.

7   Allow each pair to develop a method of recording these various combinations. For example, students might label combinations as "a-b-c" or "1-2-3" or show their combinations with different shapes.

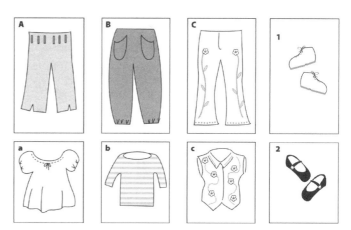

8   Stop the whole class and allow pairs to share how they're recording their possibilities. For example, the illustration at the bottom of the page shows the first step of one possible approach. Explain that students may then change their method of recording, if they want, based on the information they've gained from the other pairs.

9   At the end of the period, have pairs share their findings and compare their methods of recording.

Extensions

On another day, return to this activity. Again pair off students and then pose a question to each group. Questions could include:

- What would happen if you lost 1 of your new tops?

- Would you have been able to make more outfits with 4 shirts, 2 pairs of pants, and 2 pairs of shoes?

- What would happen if you did this with ice cream cones (6 flavors and 2 types of cones) or dolls (2 types of hair, 3 different dresses, and 2 pairs of shoes)?

COMBINATIONS

SHIRTS	C	C	C	C	C	C
PANTS	A	A	B	B	C	C
SHOES	1	2	1	2	1	2

MATH LAB OPTIONS

Differentiation is all about finding alternative pathways to learning and multiple ways for students to show what they know. In this chapter you'll find the tools you need for both, all within the math lab setting. The math lab approach is something like literacy stations; it provides differentiated opportunities for students to learn individually and in small groups. Although I've described it here in terms of something you include every day, math lab can be modified to fit whatever framework you have available. Use it daily, weekly, or even monthly—the choice is yours.

Choices can make a huge difference in your classroom, but you need a way to offer those options that doesn't require adding more hours to every day. That's where "Math Lab Choices," task cards, and the "Choice Option Menu" come in. Using these pieces as part of your math lab can save you time and assist you as you accommodate those different learners in your classroom.

The basic idea here is that every time you use math lab, each student will work on completing activities and filling in his copy of the "Math Lab Choices" reproducible to show what he's done. If appropriate, he can record his work in his mini math lab book. (Note that, in a differentiated classroom, some students may choose or be assigned tasks that take longer or are more complex. The number of choices each student completes in a given time period will vary, depending on the difficulty and complexity of the tasks and the student's ability or learning style.)

Options

There are just 2 rules for students to follow in making their choices:

1. Students may not repeat any category until they have sampled all the choices for the week. (I tell my students they need to have variety in their math diet!) So if a student works with the Math & Poetry task cards on Monday, she fills in the appropriate block for that day; she then must complete an activity in every other row before returning to the Math & Poetry task cards.

2. Each student must conference with you once a week and show you his work. That holds everybody—you *and* your students—accountable.

I want to give *you* some options, too. The task cards in this chapter give you a lot of ways to differentiate, but you can add even more if you adapt the task card activities to accommodate different levels of readiness. Here are a couple of ways to do that:

1. To make the Thrill Drill Games easier, remove all face cards and aces from each deck of cards and include only those number cards that your students can count. Or include just 2 suits (1 red and 1 black).

2. To make the Probability Cubes Games easier, have students use just 1 die, have them use lower target numbers, or decrease the number of options on the answer sheet.

Another option is to add still more variety to your math lab and encourage independence by sometimes including other activities that aren't on the "Math Lab Choices" sheet. A reproducible for a "Choice Option Menu" (page 115) will give you even more choices for your accelerated learner or one who enjoys a personal challenge.

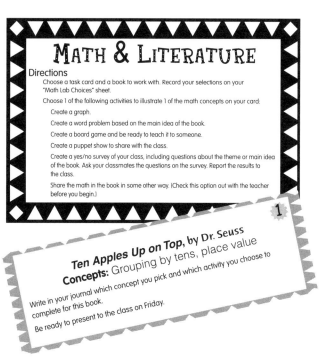

MATH & LITERATURE

Directions

Choose a task card and a book to work with. Record your selections on your "Math Lab Choices" sheet.

Choose 1 of the following activities to illustrate 1 of the math concepts on your card:

Create a graph.

Create a word problem based on the main idea of the book.

Create a board game and be ready to teach it to someone.

Create a puppet show to share with the class.

Create a yes/no survey of your class, including questions about the theme or main idea of the book. Ask your classmates the questions on the survey. Report the results to the class.

Share the math in the book in some other way. (Check this option out with the teacher before you begin.)

1

Ten Apples Up on Top, by Dr. Seuss
Concepts: Grouping by tens, place value

Write in your journal which concept you pick and which activity you choose to complete for this book.

Be ready to present to the class on Friday.

Now, let's get started!

These are the steps involved in setting up the math lab:

1. Prepare the task cards. Copy onto plain paper all of the task card reproducibles from this chapter that you want to use. Cut apart the instructions for the separate cards and attach each to a 5 x 8-inch index card, using both sides of the card when necessary. (You may want to use index cards in a different color for each set.) Laminate the cards. Punch a hole in the corner of each card and put each group of cards on a 1-inch book ring. Place each group of task cards in a bin with the appropriate materials.

2. Prepare the "Speed Racer" and "Choice Option Menu" reproducibles, adapting them if necessary for your students' needs. Copy each of these (pages 114 and 115) onto 8 1/2 x 11-inch colored card stock, again making multiple copies if you like. Laminate each copy.

3. To start off with, make at least 1 copy of the "Math Lab Choices" menu (pages 60–61) for each student in the class.

4. Gather the materials needed for each of the choices you're offering your students. To do this, work from the "Supplies" column of the "Math Lab Choices" menu and the list of "Supplies for the Math Concepts Task Cards" (page 62). You may want to photocopy the answers (page 111) for some of the task card challenges; I suggest you set the copies aside until they're needed for self-checking. The only other things you'll need are the charts referenced in the Probability Cubes Games. You'll find reproducibles for those on pages 76–77.

5. Create a math task bag for each student in your class. These bags are collections of math tools that support task card activities. For each math task bag, start with a 1-gallon resealable plastic bag. In that bag place 2 dice (each a different color), a printed 100 chart, a number line, about twenty game markers (such as dried beans or bingo markers) in a snack-size resealable plastic bag, and a deck of playing cards. Many of these items can be purchased inexpensively from dollar stores or discount online party supply sites.

6. Hand out the math task bags and give students time to explore the contents.

7. Guide students in making their first mini math lab books, so they have the books ready when they need them. For choices of formats for the mini math lab books, see pages 181–83.

8. Introduce each of the activities in a whole-group setting, modeling and then guiding students as they begin working with the materials and activities. Your students will then be familiar with your expectations when they work in small groups, in pairs, or solo.

9. Reteach as necessary in a small-group setting or with a single child. Differentiated instruction can occur with any group size. The choice is yours!

10. Identify 1 child to serve as the "banker" for the class for the first week. This student will be the keeper of the money bags used with the "Measure Up" and "Place My Value" cards and will be responsible for making sure that the bags are returned after each use with their contents intact.

11. Hand out the "Math Lab Choices" work sheets and explain to the class how your math lab will work.

12. As needed later on, introduce the "Choice Option Menu" to students who are ready for it.

MATH LAB CHOICES

	MONDAY	TUESDAY	WEDNESDAY	THURSDAY	FRIDAY	SUPPLIES
Math & Literature	Name of book: Activity:	Name of book: Activity:	Name of book: Activity:	Name of book: Activity:	Name of book: Activity:	• book named on card • math journal • writing materials • paper bag or stick puppets
Games (Thrill Drill or Probability Cubes) Write in name of game found on card.						• math task bags • work tray • mini math lab book • Fill 'Er Up chart • Refill 'Er Up chart • writing materials
Computer Game Write in name of game or Internet site.						• computer program or bookmarked Internet game • egg timer to limit the time spent
Math Concepts (Gee, I'm a Tree! or Measure Up or Place My Value)						• mini math lab book • related materials (see individual task cards)
Math Challenge (Math Strategies or Logically Speaking)						• writing materials • mini math lab book

Math & Poetry Write the name of the poem and the activity.						poetry book or card • mini math lab book • writing materials
Speed Racer Record your score.						• taped drill • tape recorder • response sheet • writing materials
Teacher Conference 1 time per week — mark the day you met with your teacher.						• mini math lab books

Supplies for the Math Concepts Task Cards

For Gee, I'm a Tree!

- geoboard
- colored rubber bands
- Wikki Stix
- mini math lab books
- pencils
- attribute blocks, purchased commercially
- graph paper
- markers
- magazines
- scissors
- glue
- construction paper
- nonflexible drinking straws
- string
- crayons
- 1-inch strips of poster board
- brads
- variety of cans & boxes
- drawing paper
- index cards
- 3-D geometric shapes, purchased commercially
- stickers
- 1-inch grid paper
- 7 tangram pieces

For Measure Up

- individual pieces of pasta
- items to measure
- pencils
- mini math lab books
- string
- scissors
- masking tape
- blocks
- digital bathroom scale
- balance scale
- items to weigh
- water or sand
- 2 clear containers of different sizes
- tray
- rubber bands
- children's cookbook
- ingredients for a recipe in the cookbook
- measuring cups and spoons
- timer
- money bag containing 20 pennies
- rubber ball
- deck of cards
- paper
- Unifix cubes

For Place My Value

- Popsicle sticks
- rubber bands or Wikki Stix
- mini math lab books
- pencils
- dry beans
- glue
- 6-inch squares of cardboard
- dice
- 2 money bags (each containing pennies, dimes, and a dollar bill)
- Unifix cubes in 3 colors
- cards numbered 1 through 9
- paper

MATH & LITERATURE

Directions

Choose a task card and a book to work with. Record your selections on your "Math Lab Choices" sheet.

Choose 1 of the following activities to illustrate 1 of the math concepts on your card:

Create a graph.

Create a word problem based on the main idea of the book.

Create a board game and be ready to teach it to someone.

Create a puppet show to share with the class.

Create a yes/no survey of your class, including questions about the theme or main idea of the book. Ask your classmates the questions on the survey. Report the results to the class.

Share the math in the book in some other way. (Check this option out with the teacher.)

Ten Apples Up on Top, by Dr. Seuss
Concepts: Grouping by tens, place value

Write in your journal which concept you pick and which activity you choose to complete for this book.

Be ready to present to the class on Friday.

The Doorbell Rang, by Pat Hutchins
Concepts: Division, sharing equally

Write in your journal which concept you pick and which activity you choose to complete for this book.

Be ready to present to the class on Friday.

How Big Is a Foot?, by Rolf Myller
Concept: Measurement of length

Write in your journal the concept listed and which activity you choose to complete for this book.

Be ready to present to the class on Friday.

A Chair for My Mother, by Vera B. Williams
Concepts: Counting, money

Write in your journal which concept you pick and which activity you choose to complete for this book.

Be ready to present to the class on Friday.

Caps for Sale, by Esphyr Slobodkina
Concepts: Patterning, counting, addition, subtraction

Write in your journal which concept you pick and which activity you choose to complete for this book.

Be ready to present to the class on Friday.

Cloudy with a Chance of Meatballs, by Judi Barrett
Concepts: Logic, measurement, patterns

Write in your journal which concept you pick and which activity you choose to complete for this book.

Be ready to present to the class on Friday.

Grandfather Tang's Story, by Ann Tompert
Concepts: Geometry, mathematical language

Write in your journal which concept you pick and which activity you choose to complete for this book.

Be ready to present to the class on Friday.

7

Who Sank the Boat?, by Pamela Allen
Concepts: Measurement, estimation, fractions

Write in your journal which concept you pick and which activity you choose to complete for this book.

Be ready to present to the class on Friday.

8

Corduroy, by Don Freeman
Concepts: Logic, attributes, measurement, place value

Write in your journal which concept you pick and which activity you choose to complete for this book.

Be ready to present to the class on Friday.

9

The Relatives Came, by Cynthia Rylant
Concepts: Statistics, estimation, problem-solving, area, measurement

Write in your journal which concept you pick and which activity you choose to complete for this book.

Be ready to present to the class on Friday.

 10

THRILL DRILL GAMES

Directions

1. Select a card for 1 of the Thrill Drill Games.
2. Enter the name of your card on the "Math Lab Choices" sheet.
3. Follow the directions on your selected card.

Players: 2–4

1

TEN IS TOPS

Goal: Be the first person to get rid of all your cards.

You'll need: 2 decks of cards with face cards removed

1. The dealer shuffles the cards and deals 7 cards to each player, then places the rest of the cards face down in a draw pile.
2. The dealer turns over the top card of the draw pile to begin the discard pile.
3. Each player looks in his hand and tries to find cards that will add up to exactly 10. (An ace is worth 1.) The player may use as many or as few cards as needed to make 10. So someone might lay down an ace and a 9 or he might lay down a 2, a 3, and a 5.

(continued on back)

4. Play begins with the person to the left of the dealer. If that player can make 10 from his cards, he lays down in front of him the set of cards that make 10. The player can lay down as many sets of 10 as he has in his hand.

5. If a player cannot make 10 from his hand, the player either draws a new card from the draw pile or takes the top card from the discard pile. He continues drawing cards until he can make 10.

6. Once the player lays down 1 or more sets of 10, his turn is over and play continues with the player to his left.

7. When there are no more cards in the draw pile, the dealer shuffles the cards in the discard pile, creates a new draw pile, and again turns over the top card to form a new discard pile.

8. Play continues until 1 player runs out of cards. That player wins the game!

Players: 2 teams of 2

2

TWENTY-FIVE TO ONE

Goal: Get a total that's lower than the other team's.

You'll need: 1 deck of cards, paper, pencil, grid based on the next task card

1. From a deck of cards, students pull out only the following cards to use in this game:

   4 of each: 2s, 3s, 4s   3 of each: 5s and 6s   1 of each: 7, 8, 9

2. A student copies the Twenty-Five to One grid (see following task card) onto a piece of paper.

3. The 2 teams place the special deck face down in the middle of the table.

(continued on back)

4. Each team draws 3 cards. The team works together to combine those numbers to add, subtract, multiply, or divide. Each answer must use either 2 or 3 of the cards. The team writes each equation in the square of the grid that contains the answer. For instance, suppose you drew the cards 6, 4, and 2. In the square containing 24 you could write "6 x 4," in the square containing 8 you could write "4 – 2 + 6," and so on.

5. Each team fills as many squares as possible, using as many different operations as possible. (Both teams do this at the same time.)

6. Each team places its 3 cards on the bottom of the pile and draws 3 more cards. They use these 3 new cards to create new combinations for any squares that are still empty.

7. Each team has 3 turns, taking 3 cards each time.

8. When each team finishes its turns, teammates add together the numbers in the squares that have no equations.

9. Teams exchange grids and check all equations. The number in any square that has an incorrect equation has to then be added to the team's score.

10. The team with the lowest total wins.

Twenty-Five to One Grid

3

Copy this grid on your paper. Use it to play Twenty-Five to One.

25	24	23	22	21
20	19	18	17	16
15	14	13	12	11
10	9	8	7	6
5	4	3	2	1

SPIT!

Goal: Be the first to get rid of all your cards.

You'll need: 1 deck of cards, face cards removed

1. The dealer shuffles and deals all the cards.
2. Players face each other, with each student's cards face down in a pile in front of him. These are the play cards.
3. From his play pile, each player draws 4 cards and places those cards face up in front of him. These are his answer cards.
4. As both say, "Spit!," each player puts out another card from his play pile and places it face up in the middle of the playing area. These are the "spit" cards.

(continued on back)

5. Each player tries to add or subtract the 2 spit cards to equal 1 of his 4 answer cards. (An ace counts as 1.)
6. Each player sets aside the answer card that showed the total for his equation and replaces it with another card from his play pile. If a player can't make an equation, he keeps all of the cards that are in his pile.
7. Both players again say, "Spit!," and each places another card from his play pile on top of the previous spit cards.
8. Play continues until 1 player runs out of cards. That player wins the game!

SNAP!
Goal: Get all the cards.
You'll need: 1 deck of cards

Players: 2

1. The dealer shuffles and deals all the cards.

2. Each player places all of her cards face down in front of her in a play pile.

3. Together, the players count, "1, 2, 3." On saying "3," each player turns over the top card in her play pile and places it in the center of the playing area.

4. Each player adds or subtracts (your choice) the 2 cards.

5. The first person who says a correct answer wins both cards.

6. Play continues until 1 player runs out of cards. That player wins the game!

Values for Cards:
Joker = 0 points
Ace = 1 point
King, Queen, Jack = 10 points
Any other card = its face value

WAR!
Goal: Get all the cards.
You'll need: 1 deck of cards

Players: 2–4

6

1. The game is played twice—once always adding and once always subtracting. Players decide whether they will be adding or subtracting for the first game. For the second game, they do the opposite.

2. The dealer shuffles and deals all cards face down.

3. Each player turns over 2 cards and adds or subtracts those 2 cards. The person who gets the higher answer (if adding) or the lower answer (if subtracting) wins all 4 cards.

4. If there is a tie, there's War! For War!, each player turns over 2 more cards and again adds or subtracts those 2 cards. This time the winner gets all the cards that are face up on the table.

5. Play continues until 1 person has all the cards. That player wins the game!

Values for Cards:
Joker = 0 points
Ace = 1 point
King, Queen, Jack = 10 points
Any other card = its face value

GO BOOM!

Goal: Be the first to get rid of all your cards and say, "Boom!"

You'll need: 1 deck of cards

1. The dealer shuffles the deck and deals 7 cards to each player. The rest of the cards become the draw pile.

2. The first person to the left of the dealer starts the play by placing 1 card from her hand face up on the table next to the draw pile. The player on her left plays a card that is the same suit or the same number. He places that card face up on top of the first card to form a discard pile. If the player cannot match the card, he must take the top card from the draw pile and continue drawing until he can play.

(continued on back)

3. When all the cards in the draw pile have been used up, the dealer shuffles the cards in the discard pile to create a new draw pile and play continues.

4. When a player places her last card on the discard pile, she calls out "Boom!" All other players must then add up the value of the cards remaining in their hands.

Values for Cards:

Joker = 0 points
Ace = 1 point
King, Queen, Jack = 10 points
Any other card = its face value

PROBABILITY CUBES GAMES

Directions

1. Get the pair of dice from your math task bag.
2. Choose a card for 1 of the Probability Cubes Games.
3. Write the name of the game you've chosen on your "Math Lab Choices" sheet.
4. Record your answers in a mini math lab book if required.

Players: 2

1

SAY IT FAST

Together, you'll need: 2 dice, a work tray, 2 mini math lab books, 2 pencils

1. Throw 1 die on the tray. "Say it fast." (Say the number on the top of the die without counting the dots!) If your partner says, "Correct," go to Step 2. If you are not correct, repeat Step 1.
2. Throw the second die and "Say it fast." If your partner says, "Correct," go to Step 3. If you are not correct, repeat Step 2.
3. Add the 2 throws together by saying the number on the first die and counting on the dots on the second die. (If your first throw was a 6 and your second throw was a 3, you would say, "6—7, 8, 9.")
4. In your mini math lab book, write down the equation that shows what you have just said (in this case, "6 + 3 = 9").
5. Trade places with your partner and let him take a turn.
6. Continue playing until each person has 6 equations in his book.

HOW MANY ROLLS TO GET A 1?

You'll need: Scratch paper, pencil, tally sheet based on the back of this task card, 1 die

1. Copy the tally sheet from the back of this task card onto your scratch paper.

2. Roll a die until a 1 comes up. Record how many rolls it took.

3. Do this 5 times.

Extension: Repeat, this time rolling for a 6. What do you notice about the results?

(continued on back)

Tally Sheet for How Many Rolls to Get a 1?

	Number of Rolls for a 1	Number of Rolls for a 6	What I Noticed
Try 1			
Try 2			
Try 3			
Try 4			
Try 5			

PIG

You'll need: 1 pair of dice to share, 1 pencil for each player, 1 mini math lab book for each player

1. The first player rolls the dice as many times as she likes.
2. She keeps a running total in her head.
3. When she decides to stop, she writes down her total in her mini math lab book and adds it to her total from previous rounds. Now it's the partner's turn to do the same thing.
4. The first player to reach 100 is the winner.
5. After you have played, write down in your mini math lab book a strategy to win.

Rules
- Careful! If a 1 comes up, your turn is over, and you get a zero for the round.
- If you get 1s on both dice on the same roll, your grand total goes to zero.

FILL 'ER UP

You'll need: 2 dice of different colors (for example, 1 red and 1 white), pencils, 1 copy of the Fill 'Er Up chart, scratch paper, 1 mini math lab book

1. One person is the recorder and the other is the roller. Each time the roller rolls the pair of dice, the recorder writes the results of that roll on the chart as an equation. For example, if the roller gets a white 1 and a red 2, the recorder writes "1 + 2 = 3" in the appropriate box.
2. On scratch paper, the roller tallies the number of rolls. If the roller rolls numbers that have already been entered in the chart, he still makes a tally mark, but the recorder does not mark anything on the chart because that box is already full.
3. Continue until there are just 5 blank boxes left.
4. In your mini math lab book, discuss how many throws it took to get that close to completing the chart. Fill in the missing sums in the chart.

REFILL 'ER UP

You'll need: 1 copy of the Refill 'Er Up chart, 1 mini math lab book, pencils

1. Complete the chart after playing Fill 'Er Up. (See back of this card for an example of how to start.)

2. In your mini math lab book, respond to the following:
   Add across the Total Ways row on the bottom. Did you get 36?
   List the possibilities from your chart, starting with the one that has the greatest probability and ending with the one that has the least probability.
   The probability of rolling a 7 is 6 chances out of 36, or 6/36, or 1/6. Why? What is the probability of rolling the other sums? Add these up. What do you notice?

(continued on back)

REFILL 'ER UP CHART

(SAMPLE STARTING POINT)

(back)

Possible Totals	2	3	4	5	6	7	8	9	10	11	12
			2,2 3,1 1,3								
Total Ways			3								

FILL 'ER UP CHART

white die →		1	2	3	4	5	6
red die ↓							
1							
2							
3							
4							
5							
6							

When there are 5 blanks left on the chart, STOP! Fill them in!

REFILL 'ER UP CHART

Possible Totals	2	3	4	5	6	7	8	9	10	11	12
Total Ways											

GEE, I'M A TREE!

Directions

1. Choose 1 of these geometry task cards.
2. On your "Math Lab Choices" sheet, write the name of the activity listed on that task card.
3. Record your answers in your mini math lab book.

Players: 1 or 2

1

GEOBOARD GEE WHIZ!

You'll need: 1 geoboard, colored rubber bands, Wikki Stix, 1 mini math lab book, pencil, attribute blocks, graph paper

1. Work alone or with a friend to explore the different shapes you can make by placing the rubber bands or the Wikki Stix around the nails on your board. How many different shapes can you make? Can you make different sizes of 1 of your shapes?
2. See how many shapes you can make with 1 rubber band. Count the sides and the number of nails you use for each shape. In your mini math lab book draw the shapes you have made.
3. Choose an attribute block. See if you can make that shape on your board with 1 rubber band. In your mini math lab book, draw the shape you have made and label it with its name.
4. On graph paper, draw the shape that you have created on your board. Be sure to connect dots and lines.

SHAPES SEARCH

Players: 1

You'll need: Markers, 1 mini math lab book, magazines, scissors, glue, construction paper

Choose **1** of these activities.

1. Take a field trip around your classroom. Find and draw in your mini math lab book as many items as you can that have the basic shapes of circle, square, triangle, rectangle, hexagon, and trapezoid.

2. Take a field trip around school. Find more examples of shapes. Draw these in a mini math lab book.

3. Choose a magazine. Cut out pictures of shapes you find in the magazine and glue them in a mini math lab book. Outline each shape with a marker.

4. Take a mini math lab book home. Look for traffic signs and other signs that use shapes. Draw them in your book. Write down where you found each one. Bring your book back to school. Use construction paper to make a copy of 1 or more of the signs you found to go on our bulletin board.

SHAPES FROM STRINGS & STRAWS

Players: 1

You'll need: 6 drinking straws, scissors, string, mini math lab book, crayons

1. Cut each straw in half. Thread the string through 3 of the straw pieces to connect them. Tighten the string, tie it, and cut it. In your mini math lab book, draw the shape you have made and label it.

2. Now do the same thing with 4 straw pieces. What have you made? Draw and label this shape in your mini math lab book.

3. Try it with 5 straw pieces. What shape does it resemble if you have 1 straw segment at the top and 2 straw segments at the bottom? Write the answer in your mini math lab book.

SWINGING SHAPES

You'll need: 1-inch-wide strips of poster board, scissors, brads

Cut strips to various lengths. Make each of these figures with your strips and brads:

1. a 3-sided figure with no sides the same length
2. a 3-sided figure with 2 sides the same length
3. a 3-sided figure with all sides the same length
4. a 4-sided figure with 2 pairs of sides the same length
5. a figure with more than 4 sides all the same length
6. a figure with 6 sides all the same length

CAN IT, BOX IT, DRAW IT

You'll need: Assorted cans and boxes, drawing paper, pencil

1. Find as many different shapes of cans and boxes as you can.
2. Place each one on your drawing paper. Trace around the base of each container onto the paper.
3. Write the name of each shape next to the drawing you have made.
4. Add size words to your drawings to show which drawing is the smallest, which is the largest, and which ones are medium-size.
5. Can you combine some of the shapes to make a picture on another sheet of paper?

SOMETIMES YOU'RE RIGHT. SOMETIMES YOU'RE NOT!

You'll need: Pencil, index card, mini math lab book

1. Label 1 corner of your index card as "right angle." This is your "angle card."
2. Use your angle card to explore the corners in our classroom.
3. When you find a right angle that fits your card, stop and draw in your mini math lab book a picture of where you are.
4. In your mini math lab book, write the name of what you have just drawn.
5. Check out other places and things in our room that have right angles. List those in your mini math lab book, along with a drawing of each one.

Players: 1

GETTING THE RIGHT ANGLE

You'll need: Scissors, construction paper, glue

1. Cut out different sizes of squares from different colors of construction paper. Cut each square apart on the diagonal (corner to corner). You have now made right triangles! Count how many right angles you have made.
2. Combine your right triangles into designs on another sheet of construction paper. Glue them in place.

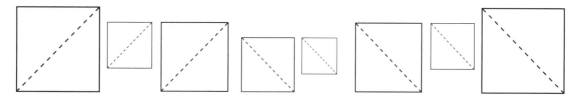

SOLID, JACKSON

8

You'll need: 3-D geometric shapes, mini math lab book, pencil

1. Place the solid shapes on the table. See which of the shapes answers each of the following riddles:

   a. This solid is flat all over and each side is the same. It is a _____.

   b. This solid is flat on the bottom and its sides are triangles. It is a _____.

   c. This solid is flat on the bottom, the sides are smooth, and the top has a point. It is a_____.

   d. This solid has smooth sides and both ends are flat. It is a_____.

   e. This solid is smooth and is round all over. It is a_____.

2. In your mini math lab book, draw the solids you used and write down what you discovered about each one.

3. In your mini math lab book, write down where you might see each of these solids in the "real world." Next to each listing, draw a picture of the real-world object you've named.

Players: 1

9

CAN THIS BE TRUE!

You'll need: Scissors, string, assorted sizes of cans, mini math lab book, marker, pencil

1. Cut a string that is just long enough to go around 1 of your small cans.

2. Use the string you just cut to measure how tall the can is. Compare the can's height to its "circumference" (the length of the string or the distance around the can). In your mini math lab book, write down what you notice.

3. Number the rest of your cans. Write the numbers in your mini math lab book.

4. For the next can, cut a piece of string that will just go around that can. But this time, before you actually measure the height of the can, predict how the length of your string will compare with the can's height. Then write what you find when you measure.

(continued on back)

5. Repeat the process for each of the remaining cans. For each can, write your prediction next to the appropriate number in your mini math lab book before you measure the can's height.

Extension: Find other cylinder containers (glasses, jars, cups, waste baskets, and so on) in your classroom. For each container, repeat the process of drawing, predicting, and measuring that you used for the cans. In your mini math lab book, write what you've noticed about the distance around a container compared to its height.

`Players: 1`

SYMMETRY SAMPLES

10

You'll need: Assorted colors of construction paper, markers, scissors, stickers

1. Fold 1 of the pieces of paper in half. On the fold, draw half of 1 of these figures:

- House
- Butterfly
- Heart
- Square
- Fish
- Rectangle
- Kite
- Triangle
- Oval
- Your choice

2. Cut out the figure, cutting through both layers, and unfold your paper.
3. Now use the markers and stickers to decorate your figure—keeping the symmetry! Whatever you do on 1 side of the fold needs to be copied on the other side of the fold.

SIMPLY SYMMETRY

You'll need: 1-inch grid paper, markers, mini math lab book

1. Take a piece of grid paper and fold it in half.
2. Draw half of a shape on the fold.
3. Unfold the paper.
4. Invite a friend to draw the other half.
5. Count how many grid squares you each used. What do you notice?
6. Record your observations in your mini math lab book.

Players: 1

TAN, TAN, TANGRAM

You'll need: 1 set of 7 tangram pieces, markers, mini math lab book

1. Use the 3 smallest triangles to make:

   • A triangle   • A square   • A rectangle   • A trapezoid   • A parallelogram
   Draw each one in your mini math lab book and record how you made it.

2. Use the 5 smallest pieces (not the 2 large triangles) and make the same 5 shapes you made in Step 1. Draw each one in your mini math lab book and record how you made it.

3. Now use all the pieces and make these same shapes. Again draw each one in your mini math lab book and record how you made it.

Bonus: Create a picture using your 7 tangram pieces. Be sure they touch! Draw around the 7 pieces on a sheet of paper, but don't show the lines between the pieces. Name your picture and place it on the bulletin board. Let your friends try to figure out how you created your picture.

MEASURE UP

Directions

1. Choose 1 of the task cards.
2. On your "Math Lab Choices" sheet, write the number of the activity listed on that task card.
3. Record your answers in your mini math lab book.

As you work with these task cards, keep 2 guidelines in mind:

1. Be sure the units you use to measure are the same size.
2. Be sure the units you use to measure are touching each other.

REMEMBER: Measuring can be done with just about anything—not just rulers or measuring cups!

Players: 1

PASTA PARTY

1

You'll need: Pieces of pasta (all the same kind and size), something to measure (scissors, shoe, etc.), pencil, mini math lab book

1. Line up your first pasta piece evenly with the end of whatever you are measuring. Lay the rest of the pasta pieces so they touch each other and follow the line of the object you are measuring. Keep laying down pasta pieces until you reach the end of the object.
2. Count how many pieces of pasta you have used.
3. Write the answer in your mini math lab book.

If your pasta doesn't exactly line up with what you're measuring at the other end, stop! It's okay. You will have a "between." Let's say you are measuring a pencil, and the lined-up pasta pieces don't match the length of your pencil. You write down, "My pencil is between 5 and 6 pieces of pasta."

STRING ME ALONG

You'll need: String, scissors, pencil, mini math lab book

1. Ask your partner to cut a string as long as you are tall.
2. With your partner's help, use the string to compare the lengths of your different body parts.
3. Finish these sentences, writing each one in your mini math lab book:

The string went around my head ___ times.

The string went across my foot ___ times.

The string went around my waist ___ times.

The string went across my arm ___ times.

The string went _____ (your choice) ___ times.

HOW MANY STUDENTS?

You'll need: Friends, pencil, mini math lab book

1. Join hands with your friends and see how many students it takes to go across the classroom.
2. Now use your friends to measure the distance between the other 2 walls in the classroom in the same way. What did you notice?
3. Record your observations in your mini math lab book.

TOE-HEEL WALK

You'll need: Scissors, masking tape, 1 friend, pencil, mini math lab book

1. Cut pieces of masking tape in different lengths and stick them to the floor.
2. Do a heel-toe walk along the tape (making sure the heel of your front foot touches the toe of your back foot with each step) and compare the number of footsteps it takes for each strip.
3. Ask someone else to walk the strips. Are your footstep numbers the same? Why or why not? Talk about any differences.
4. Write about your discoveries in your mini math lab book.

FRIENDS ON THE FLOOR

You'll need: Classroom blocks (all the same size), pencil, mini math lab book, 5 friends

1. Have 1 friend lie on the floor.
2. Measure this friend's height using classroom blocks. Count the number of blocks used.
3. In your mini math lab book, record your friend's name and how many blocks tall he is.
4. Repeat with 4 other friends.
5. In your mini math lab book, write what you notice about any differences. ("Johnny is 3 blocks taller than Suzy.")

DIGITAL DOINGS

You'll need: Digital bathroom scale, pencil,
mini math lab book, 5 friends

1. Find and record the weights of 5 friends.
2. Make up some comparison statements and write them in your mini math lab book ("John weighs 5 pounds more than Susan. Susan weighs 3 pounds less than Adam.")

BALANCES OUT

You'll need: Classroom blocks, balance scale, classroom
items to weigh (books, rulers, stapler, etc.), pencil,
mini math lab book

1. Choose a block from the classroom.
2. Place the block on 1 side of the scale.
3. Find things in the classroom that are heavier than, lighter than, and the same weight as the block.
4. Record your findings in your mini math lab book. ("The block was heavier than my book. My shoe was heavier than the block. My pencil box weighed the same as the block.")

WATER OR SAND PLAY

You'll need: Water or sand (not both), 2 clear containers of different sizes, tray, rubber band, pencil, mini math lab book

1. Pour the water or sand into the smaller container.
2. Set the other materials on the tray.
3. Estimate where on the larger container the level will be when you pour the water or sand from the smaller container into the larger one.
4. Wrap the rubber band around the container to show where the water or sand level will be.
5. Pour the water or sand into the larger container and compare your estimate to the results.
6. Write your conclusions in your mini math lab book.

COOKING UP DELICIOUS MATH

You'll need: Cookbook, pencil, mini math lab book, cooking ingredients, measuring cups and spoons

1. Look in the cookbook. Find a recipe that you can make for a group of friends in your class.
2. Copy the recipe in your mini math lab book.
3. Follow the directions and make the recipe.
4. What math did you use? (Amounts of ingredients? Measurements of dry ingredients or wet ingredients? Time to prepare or to cook? Heat for baking? Fractional parts?) Write the answer(s) in your mini math lab book.
5. What would your recipe look like if you doubled it so that it could serve more people? Write the new recipe in your mini math lab book. Tell how many people you think this new recipe will serve.

MIND YOUR MINUTES

You'll need: 1 timer, 20 pennies or a playground rubber ball, 2 mini math lab books, 2 pencils, coin

1. Choose 1 of these tasks and have your partner time you as you complete it:
   - Place 20 pennies 1 at a time in a glass.
   - Bounce a ball 20 times.
   - Your choice.

   In your mini math lab book, write,

   "It took me_____ minutes to _____."

(continued on back)

2. Ask your friend with the timer to tell you when 3 minutes are up. See how many times you can do each of these things in 3 minutes:

   - Walk across the classroom.
   - Crawl across the classroom.
   - Walk backward across the classroom.
   - Walk sideways across the classroom.
   - Hop across the classroom.

   - Flip a coin.
   - Blink your eyes.
   - Snap your fingers.
   - Tap your toes.
   - Clap your hands.

3. Swap roles with your partner and repeat Steps 1 and 2.

VARIATION: Try other times (both longer and shorter) for Step 2. Keep track of the results in your mini math lab book. What happens as your time limits change?

YOU'RE A CARD

You'll need: Deck of cards, pencil, mini math lab book

1. The goal is to use a deck of cards to cover the area of several flat surfaces in our room.
2. Start with your desk. Place the cards in straight rows across the desk. Cover the desk with touching rows of cards.
3. Count the number of cards it takes to cover your desk. Record that number in your mini math lab book.
4. Repeat with other desks and tables in our classroom. Try to find ones that are different sizes. In your mini math lab book, write the name of each desk or table ("Juan's desk," "Mrs. Wright's table") and the number of cards you used to cover it.

NO MEAN FEET

You'll need: Paper, pencil, Unifix cubes, mini math lab book

1. Place your foot on the paper and draw around your shoe with a pencil.
2. Remove your foot from the paper.
3. Fill your foot outline on the paper with Unifix cubes. This is the "area" of your foot.
4. Write the result in your mini math lab book. ("The area of my foot is ___ cubes.")
5. Now place Unifix cubes around the edges of your foot's outline. Be sure they touch!
6. Count how many cubes it took to go around the outline. This is the "perimeter" of your foot.
7. Write this result in your mini math lab book. ("The perimeter of my foot is ___ cubes.")
8. Write in your lab book what you notice about the difference between the 2 numbers. ("The area of my foot is ___ than the perimeter.")

PLACE MY VALUE

Directions

1. Begin with task card #1.
2. On your "Math Lab Choices" sheet, write the number of the activity listed on your task card.
3. Record your answers in your mini math lab book.
4. Work the rest of the cards in order. Feel free to repeat or go back to a card that you have already worked.

Players: 1

1

BUNDLES & LEFTOVERS

You'll need: Popsicle sticks with rubber bands or Wikki Stix to hold the bundles together, mini math lab book, pencil

1. Pick a number from the row at the bottom of this card.
2. Count out the Popsicle sticks you need to make the number. From those sticks, create as many bundles of 10 sticks as you can.
3. Place your "leftover" sticks next to the bundles.
4. In your mini math lab book, draw a picture of what you did and write the number you chose.

For example: If you had the number 57, you would have 5 bundles of 10 sticks and 7 leftover sticks.

| 12 | 31 | 72 | 24 | 39 | 25 | 68 | 16 |

NAME THAT BUNDLE!

You'll need: Popsicle sticks with rubber bands or Wikki Stix to hold the bundles together, pencil, mini math lab book

1. Use the sticks and bands or Wikki Stix to match the pictures on the back of this card. Each bundle should include 10 Popsicle sticks.
2. Write the number for each bundle picture in your mini math lab book.
3. Make up your own combination of bundles and sticks. In your mini math lab book, draw a picture of what you've made up. Next to your picture, write the number for your combination.

(continued on back)

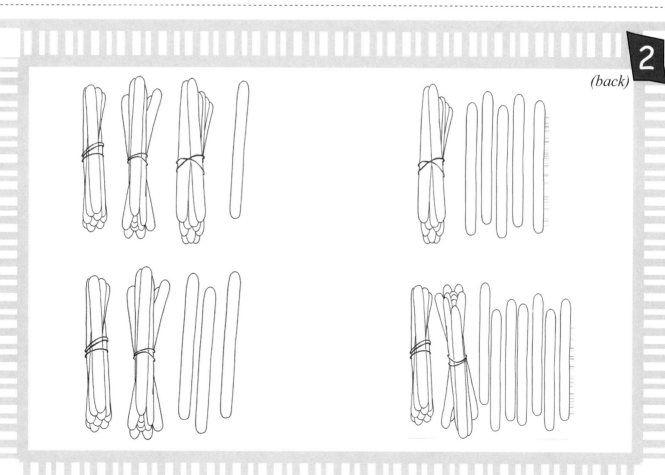

BUNDLE TAKE AWAY

You'll need: Popsicle sticks with rubber bands or Wikki Stix to hold the bundles together, pencil, mini math lab book

1. Go to the first row on the back of this card, and show the first number in bundles and leftovers.
2. Still working in the same row, take away enough sticks to show the second number (for 33, you would take away 3 bundles and 3 leftovers).
3. Write the first number, the take-away number, and the new number in your mini math lab book.
4. Make up your own combination of numbers. Write the first number, the take-away number, and the new number in your mini math lab book.

(continued on back)

3

(back)

Hint: You may have to take the bands off the bundles and then re-bundle into 10s and singles again.

First number	Take away	New number
45	33	_____
52	17	_____
43	27	_____
64	45	_____

BUNDLE UP

You'll need: Popsicle sticks with rubber bands or Wikki Stix to hold the bundles together, mini math lab book, pencil

1. Go to the first row on the back of this card, and make the first number in bundles and leftovers.
2. Now show the second number in the same row with a different set of bundles and leftovers.
3. Look at all of your leftovers. Do you have at least 10 leftovers? Can you combine these leftovers to make another bundle of 10?
4. Count the number of bundles and leftovers. Write in your mini math lab book the new number you have made.
5. Repeat for each of the other rows.

(continued on back)

First number	Second number	New number
23	45	_____
17	36	_____
37	26	_____
52	28	_____

Now, make up your own number for each column and combine them to figure out the new number you have made.

PICTURE THIS!

You'll need: Popsicle sticks with rubber bands or Wikki Stix to hold the bundles together, mini math lab book, pencil

1. Solve each of the addition problems on this card using bundles and leftovers.
2. In your mini math lab book, draw pictures of what you have done.
3. Write your equation, including the answer, in your mini math lab book.
4. Now, make up 3 new number sentences and create some new equations. Write your equations, including the answers, in your mini math lab book.

$28 + 26 =$ $35 + 17 =$

$43 + 22 =$ $56 + 19 =$

MORE PICTURES!

You'll need: Popsicle sticks with rubber bands or Wikki Stix to hold the bundles together, mini math lab book, pencil

1. Solve the subtraction problems on this card with bundles and leftovers. Start with the first number and take away the second number.
2. In your mini math lab book, write the equation to show what you did in each case and how many bundles and leftovers you ended up with.
3. Now, make up 3 new number sentences and create some new equations.

$78 - 23 =$ $53 - 26 =$

$88 - 38 =$ $78 - 49 =$

RACE FOR A FLAT

Goal: Be the first to get enough longs to trade for a flat.

You'll need: Dry beans, Popsicle sticks, glue, 6-inch square of cardboard, 1 die from your math task bag, mini math lab book

Preparation: Each of you needs to make 9 long sticks and 1 flat for this game. To make a long stick, glue 10 dry beans to 1 Popsicle stick. To make a flat, make 10 longs and glue them to a square of cardboard.

(continued on back)

 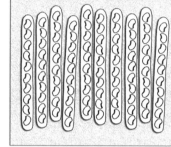

UNIT   LONG   FLAT

Once your longs and flats are ready, each of you should go to your mini math lab book and draw 3 columns like this:

F (Flat)	L (Longs)	U (Units)
	(Nine is fine!)	(Nine is fine!)

Now you are ready to play!

1. Each player rolls 1 die. The person who rolls the higher number takes the first turn.

2. On the first turn, player 1 rolls the die and puts 1 bean in the "U" column of his paper for every dot shown on the die. For instance, if player 1 rolls a 5, he puts 5 beans in the "U" column.

3. Player 2 now rolls the die and puts that number of beans in her "U" column.

4. Continue as above. When a player gets more than 9 beans in the "U" column, it is time to trade 10 beans in for a "long" that goes in the "L" column. Only 9 beans can go in the "U" column. (Nine is fine!)

5. When a player gets more than 9 longs, that player trades 10 longs for a flat and wins the game!

RACE FOR A DOLLAR

Goal: Be the first to get enough dimes to trade for a dollar.

You'll need: 1 die, 2 money bags from the "banker," mini math lab book

1. Copy the chart on the back of this card into your mini math lab book.
2. Each player rolls 1 die. The person who rolls the higher number takes the first turn.
3. Player 1 rolls the die and puts 1 penny on the chart for every dot on the die.
4. Player 2 does the same thing.
5. When a player gets more than 9 pennies, it is time to trade 10 pennies in for a dime. Remember: Nine is fine!

(continued on back)

---

6. The first person to get more than 9 dimes gets to trade 10 dimes in for a dollar and wins the game!
7. Count the money to make sure nothing is missing. Return the money bag to the banker.

$ Dollar $	Dimes	Pennies
	(Nine is fine!)	(Nine is fine!)

VARIATION: Try going from a dollar down to a penny. The first player starts with a dollar. Each player rolls the die and subtracts the number he gets from $1. He uses dimes and pennies to show the new number. Players take turns rolling the die and subtracting the amount until 1 player gets to 0. The first player to get to 0 or below wins!

Players: 2

9

FIX ME UP

Goal: Be the first to get 10 tens cubes to trade for 1 hundreds cube.

You'll need: 1 die from your math task bag, 3 colors of Unifix cubes that snap together

1. Players decide which color Unifix cube they want to use for the ones, which color will be the tens, and which color will be the hundreds.
2. Each player rolls 1 die. The person who rolls the higher number takes the first turn.
3. Player 1 rolls the die. She puts a ones cube on the table for each dot on the die, stacks those cubes, and connects all of those cubes together.

(continued on back)

9

(back)

4. Player 2 takes a turn rolling and stacking.
5. Players continue taking turns as above.
6. When a player gets more than 9 ones cubes, it is time to trade 10 ones cubes for a tens cube. Remember: Nine is fine! You can connect only 9 cubes before you need to trade to the next color.
7. The first person to get more than 9 tens cubes can trade in 10 tens cubes for a hundreds cube. That person wins the game!

DITCH A NUMBER

Goal: Come up with the higher number and beat your partner.

For each player, you'll need: Set of cards numbered 1 through 9, paper, pencil

Game Preparation: Each player draws 3 boxes of equal size on a sheet of paper. Under the last box on the right, he draws 1 more box the same size as the others. This is the "ditch" box.

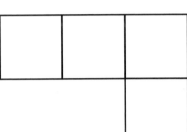

(continued on back)

---

1. Player 1 turns over 1 of his cards and writes the number on the card in any box on his paper.

2. Player 2 turns over 1 of her cards and writes the number in any box on her paper.

3. Players continue taking turns turning over cards and filling boxes until every box (including the ditch box) contains 1 number. Only 1 number can go in a box—including the ditch box. Once a number has been placed, it **cannot be moved!**

4. After each player turns over 4 cards, players look at the numbers they've created and decide who has the greater number. For instance, if your 3 boxes have the numerals 5, 4, and 6 with 1 in your ditch box, you have created the numeral 546. If your friend has the numerals 9, 7, and 3 with 8 in his ditch box, he has created the greater number of 973 and he wins the game.

5. Students play 5 times and see who wins the most games.

VARIATION: Draw 4 boxes (plus a ditch box) to include the thousands place.

MATH STRATEGIES

Directions

1. Select 1 of the Math Strategies task cards.
2. Enter the number of your challenge on the "Math Lab Choices" work sheet.
3. Follow the directions on your selected card.

Subproblems

Share & Share Alike

Three children decided to have a party and to share the expenses equally. Kate spent $3 for ice cream. Maria bought a cake for $5, and Nancy bought $1 worth of candy. How much did each person pay the others so that each of them spent the same amount?

Hints: How much was spent by all? How much was each child's share?

Diagrams

Mixed up Coins

My brother was playing around with the money from his allowance and left the coins on his bed in 4 rows with 4 coins in each row. Each row had just 1 penny, 1 nickel, 1 dime, and 1 quarter. How were they arranged if no row and no column had more than 1 kind of coin?

Hint: Using real objects and moving them around is easier than erasing!

Smaller Numbers

The Wedding Feast

The king decided to put on a great wedding feast for his princess. He had 17 tables that each had 10 plates of ham. He had 36 tables that each had 14 plates of roast beef, and he had 50 tables that each had 25 plates of vegetables. How many plates were needed to serve the ham, beef, and vegetables?

Hint: Begin by making it easier. Use smaller numbers. Also, forget about the vegetables! What would he need for 2 tables with 4 plates of ham each and 3 tables with 3 plates of roast beef each?

4

Patterns

Wizard's Road

We are planning to do a play about the Wizard of Oz at school. We want to make the yellow brick road from 18 x 24-inch paper. We need to tape the sheets of paper together on the 24-inch edges. How much tape do we need for a 10-foot-long road?

We also need to tape the paper to the floor of the stage. How much tape will we need to tape around the outside of the papers?

Hints: Draw a chart to help you. Also, try using easier numbers first. How much tape would it take to go around 1 sheet of paper?

Working Backward

Playing Monopoly

We were playing Monopoly at school. Not long after starting, I had to give up half of my money to pay for hotels. Then I had to pay $100 to get out of jail. And then I lost half of the money I had left. By the time this round was over, I had $200 left. How much did I start this round with?

Hints: What did the player have left at the end of the round? Start with that number and go back through the story. Also, try using smaller numbers at first.

Multiple Solutions

Pizza Panic

The class was having a special pizza party at school. There were 30 kids who were hungry and each kid was ready for his own special piece of pizza. The teacher was planning to cut each of the 5 pizzas into 6 slices when she realized 1 of the pizzas was not yet cooked. She decided she needed to cut some of the cooked pizzas into 7 pieces and some into 8 pieces so that she would have enough for each student. How many pizzas would need to be cut in 6 pieces? 7 pieces? 8 pieces?

(continued on back)

(back)

Hints: Start by figuring out how many pieces she'd get if she cut each pizza into 6 pieces. How many more pieces does she need, and how can she get them? Make a chart to help you decide the possibilities.

Extension: What if the teacher had already cut 1 of the 5 pizzas?

LOGICALLY SPEAKING

Directions

1. Select a task card. On your "Math Lab Choices" work sheet, enter the number of the challenge you've chosen.

(continued on back)

(back)

2. Try as many different ways as you need to in order to solve your challenge. You may work with a partner, draw diagrams, create graphs, use real items, or try any other way that works for you.

3. Talk with someone else who selected the same challenge. Compare and contrast how each of you solved the problem.

4. Record your thinking in your mini math lab book or illustrate your solution on a large poster that you can share with the whole class.

1

Dad's Age & Mine

My father's age I just found out;
He's 4 times as old as me.
But after only 5 more years,
His age will be mine times 3.

2

What Are the Odds?

Write 4 different odd numbers that add up to exactly 20.

Triangular Addition

Arrange the digits 1 through 9 along the sides of a triangle so that the numbers on each side (including the numbers at the corners) add up to 17.

Count Again

Looking out the window, I saw an assortment of boys and dogs.
Counting heads, I got 22. Counting legs, I got 68.
How many boys were in the yard? How many dogs?

How Old Are the Children?

The father was asked the exact ages of his 2 children.
He couldn't remember, but he said,
"If you subtract 1 age from the other you get 2.
When you multiply their ages you get 99."
What are the children's ages?

Puzzling Columns

Move just 1 number to a different column and then all the columns will have the same sum.

A	B	C
1	4	7
2	5	8
3	6	9
6	15	24

Sign Here!

Fill in the correct signs (+, −, x, ÷) on the back of this task card to have all the statements make sense.

(continued on back)

| 8 | 7 | 12 | = | 44 | | 4 | 3 | 4 | = | 28 |

| 7 | 5 | 6 | = | 12 | | 25 | 9 | 10 | = | 6 |

| 4 | 4 | 16 | = | 32 | | 50 | 2 | 5 | = | 20 |

Hand Over Hand

How many times do the hands of the clock cross each other in 12 hours?

Prove Your Age

Multiply the number 9 by any other number lower than 9.
Subtract this product from 10 times your age.
The first digit plus the last digit gives you your age.
Why does this work?

MATH & POETRY

Directions:

Select a poem. On your "Math Lab Choices" work sheet, write the name of the poem and the activity you've chosen.

Find instances where any of these math concepts are used:
- Measurement • Time • Money • Patterns • Number operations (+, −, x, ÷)

In your mini math lab book, list:

Name of poem   Name of poet   Name and page number of the book

In your mini math lab book, respond to the following:

Tell how numbers or math concepts are used in this poem.

Write out any computation that is talked about in the poem or draw an illustration showing the math in the poem. Was the math reasoning in the poem logical? Why or why not?

(See the back of this task card for an example.)

(back)

Sample Student Response

Name of Poem: Three Little Kittens
Name of Poet: Mother Goose
Book: Mother Goose Rhymes, page 10

Used concept of counting by 2s
2 + 2 + 2 = 6 lost mittens
Yes, the reasoning was logical.

from *Where the Sidewalk Ends,*
by Shel Silverstein

- Smart
- Band Aids
- The Gypsies Are Coming
- Me and My Giant
- For Sale
- One Inch Tall
- Lester

from *A Light in the Attic,*
by Shel Silverstein

How Many, How Much
Homework Machine
Overdues

Shapes
Kidnapped

from *Bing Bang Boing,*
by Douglas Florian

What a Mad Magician Did to Me
My Building
What I Want for My Birthday

Squares
What the Garbage Truck Ate for
Breakfast Today

from *The New Kid on the Block,*
by Jack Prelutsky

I Am Falling Off a Mountain
Forty Performing Bananas
Suzanna Socked Me Sunday

An Alley Cat with One Life Left
Ounce and Bounce

from *If You're Not Here, Please Raise Your Hand*, by Kalli Dakos

- Math Is Brewing and I'm in Trouble
- A Day in School
- It's Inside My Sister's Lunch
- They Don't Do Math in Texas

from *Lunch Money & Other Poems About School*, by Carol Diggory Shields

Eight-Oh-Three
Lunch Money
Math My Way

Clock-Watching
Book Report

MORE POETRY

Create your own math and poetry card with poetry you have found or have written.

If you are writing a poem, include math reasoning or different math concepts. Your reasoning can be true or false.

(continued on back)

(back)

If you have found a poem, write down the poet's name. If it's a short poem, copy it. If it's a long poem, ask the teacher to copy it for you.

Be ready to share your thinking with the class.

Probability Cubes
Games: Refill 'Er Up

Possible Totals	2	3	4	5	6	7	8	9	10	11	12
	1,1	2,1	2,2	2,3	1,5	5,2	4,4	3,6	5,5	5,6	6,6
		1,2	3,1	5,1	2,4	2,5	3,5	6,3	6,4	6,5	
			1,3	4,1	3,3	4,3	5,3	4,5	4,6		
				1,4	4,2	1,5	2,6	5,4			
						5,1	6,2				
						3,4					
Total Ways	1	2	3	4	5	6	5	4	3	2	1

Gee, I'm a Tree!: Solid, Jackson
8
  a. cube
  b. pyramid
  c. cone
  d. cylinder
  e. sphere

Logically Speaking

1   Pa is 40 and I am 10.

2   1, 3, 7, 9 or 1, 3, 5, 11

3
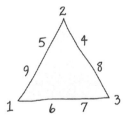

4   10 boys, 12 dogs

5   9 and 11

6   Move the 9 from Column C to Column A.

7   8 x 7 − 12, 4 + 3 x 4, 7 − 5 x 6, 25 − 9 − 10, 4 x 4 + 16, 50 x 2 ÷ 5

8   12 times: 1:05, 2:11, 3:16, . . .

9   Answer varies

Speed Racer

Speed Racer is a fun-packed, fast-paced, math-fact fluency drill. It can be played in pairs, in a small group, or with the whole class. It can be used to practice addition, subtraction, or multiplication. Each student's "race number" is based on the fact family he's working on, but students with different race numbers can still listen to and respond to the same tape at the same time.

MATERIALS

FOR EACH STUDENT

- 1 copy of the "Speed Racer" reproducible (page 114)

FOR EACH GROUP

- Tape recorder
- Cassette tape

Teacher Prep

Before class, make enough copies of the "Speed Racer" reproducible so that each player can have 1. Also, prepare an audio tape that gives only random numbers, carefully spaced on the tape to give the students time to write down each equation. The tape should have 3 segments, each with 9 random numbers. Be sure to designate each segment as Trial 1, 2, or 3.

Directions

1. Give each student a copy of the "Speed Racer" reproducible.

2. At the bottom of his sheet, each student fills in his name and "race number." The race number is the math fact family that the student is working on. For instance, if a student is struggling with +9, then +9 would be his race number. Another student might be struggling with −3, so her race number would be −3.

3. Students listen to the teacher-prepared audio tape. As a student hears each random number, he creates an equation in the column under Trial 1 using the random number and his race number. So if the student hears "7" and his race number is +9, he writes his equation in the first box as 7 + 9 = 16. In

the next box, under Trial 1 he writes the equation for his race number and the next random number heard on the tape. He must complete writing down the entire equation, including the answer, before the next random number is read.

4. At the end of the drill, students stop the tape. Each player trades papers with a partner and partners check each other's work. (Alternatively, a student can use a calculator to check her own answers.)

5. Students enter the number of correct answers on the Score line under Trial 1. Any incomplete equations do not count toward the score, but should be completed before the next trial in order to help students improve their speed.

6. Students turn the tape back on and repeat the process for Trial 2 and Trial 3.

Variation

Supply a second tape with a faster tempo for those who would like to speed up their response times.

SPEED RACER
Student Response Sheet

Trial 1	Trial 2	Trial 3

Score_____   Score_____   Score_____

Student name: _____ Race number:_____

CHOICE OPTION MENU FOR MULTIPLE INTELLIGENCES

Student:_____

Topic:_____

Date: _____ Date due:_____

Choose 4 activities that you can complete to show what you've learned. If you prefer, you may list as your fourth option something that isn't on the chart, but you'll need your teacher's permission for that. Write 1 choice on each line.

1. _____   3. _____

2. _____   4. _____

Teacher okay for alternative choice: _____

Word Smart Prepare a math lesson to teach to the class. Involve the other students. You may make up a game, graph, or glyph; start a discussion; or find another way to involve the class.	**Compare & Contrast** Create 2 ways to solve a math problem from real life. Is 1 better than the other? Show why or why not.
Picture Smart Create a visual for a presentation of your math reasoning. This can be computer generated, your own art, or something you've found.	**Number Smart** Create a graphic organizer, poster, manipulative, or computer-generated display to show how to solve a real-life math problem.
Body Smart Make up a play, a reader's theater, a dramatic reading, or a pantomime to show how to solve a math problem. Or act out the problem as if you were playing Charades and let the class guess what you're showing.	**People Smart** Create a survey and ask other students to answer the questions on your survey. Create a graphic to share the results.
	Show What You Know Create an unusual way to share your math knowledge. You may use music, rap, or rhyme.
Think Smart Invent a math problem. How could the solution to your math problem change in 20 years? Create a mock newscast or newspaper to share your ideas.	**Go Beyond Books** Conduct and tape an interview with an expert on a math problem. Add written comments on what you found out.

TASK CARDS FOR REAL-WORLD MATH

Students need to know that math matters, that it's more than just a work sheet that's completed and left at school or posted on the refrigerator at home. They need to know that math can help them in the real world when they want to place an order at a restaurant, plan a trip, shop for groceries or new clothes, compare sports scores, or order gifts by mail—especially when they have a limited amount of money. Seen in context like this, adding and subtracting suddenly become much more important to the young mathematician.

This ties into the basis of differentiated learning—the fact that children come to us with different backgrounds, different abilities, and different interests. Some students already have the background knowledge to understand how math can help them in the real world. Some have already had practice with real-world applications (deciding how to spend a specific amount of birthday money, for example). For many students, though, the chance to try out math skills in real-world situations can expand much-needed background knowledge, dramatically elevate interest, and stimulate important connections between math class and the outside world.

Tiering (Multilevel Instruction)

Basic to differentiating instruction is the opportunity to tier instruction. This means that with different levels (tiers) in our classrooms, we can provide different opportunities for students to practice and review the information that we've initially presented in a more structured setting. Recognizing that students have different levels of skills and understanding, we can tier our lessons to reach each child at her own level.

These task cards offer you a great way to do just that. The objectives and standards stay the same for each student, but you can accommodate individuals by giving them practice opportunities that are meaningful to them and allow them to find success. Practice helps all students move new information into long-term memory.

There are 2 sets of cards in this section. The set that begins on page 120 is for children who are working at or above grade level. The set that begins on page 124 is for younger learners and for children whose skills are not yet at grade level.

Assembling Materials

To introduce real-world math, you need to introduce reading materials that include numbers from the real world. That can include the books and magazines from your classroom library, but you can greatly enrich your students' experiences with real-world math if you go beyond those basics. The activities on these task cards call for students to work with restaurant menus, road maps, and pictures and descriptions from advertising flyers and catalogs. These materials are usually not hard to come by, especially if you enlist parents to help accumulate them. You'll need the following:

- Newspapers, including sports pages with statistics for teams and players
- Magazines
- Restaurant menus
- Road maps with legends showing the scale for distance (try contacting your state's department of transportation)
- Clear plastic money jar or resealable plastic bag containing real coins (or play money)
- Unifix cubes
- Calculators
- Mall ads or sales flyers from local stores
- Grocery store flyers (try for flyers from more than 1 store for comparison shopping)
- Gift catalogs
- Shipping and handling charts that list these fees as dollar amounts, not percentages

Preparing the Task Cards

1. Copy all the task card reproducibles from this chapter onto plain paper. Cut apart the instructions for the separate cards and attach each to a 5 x 8-inch index card, using both sides of the card when necessary. If you're using both sets of cards, you may want to use blue stock for the cards that begin on page 120 and green stock for the cards that begin on page 124.

2. Cut the cards apart and laminate them.

3. Hole punch the cards and group them together on 1-inch book rings.

4. Feel free to add more task cards created by you or your students to truly differentiate your instruction.

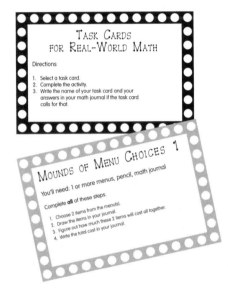

Teacher Tip

Have 1 child act as "banker for the week." That child is responsible for keeping track of how much money is taken out of the money jar and for making sure that all of it comes back.

Putting It All Together

1. Set up a tub(s) or small boxes with the materials described. Place similar resources together. (You might have maps in 1 tub, menus in another, and brochures in another.)

2. Hang the task card rings from hooks or place them in a separate box or small tub.

3. Place the tub(s) and task cards in your math lab area. If you're using both sets of cards, it's a good idea to store each set in a different area of the classroom to avoid confusion.

4. Have these tubs and task cards available during exploration time, centers time, and independent work time.

Implementing the Task Cards

1. Each student chooses a task card from the appropriate set (without removing the card from the ring).
2. The student selects what he needs from the tub containing the appropriate related material. (If he chooses a task card that calls for a menu, then he must choose a menu and not a map to complete the activity.)
3. If the task card calls for it, the student records his responses in a math journal.
4. During group sharing time, students report what they've learned.
5. Together, you and each student select some of these written responses to become part of that child's individual portfolio.

Real-World Math Made Easier

If you're using the easier task cards for younger or less ready learners, you'll need to modify some of your materials to accommodate the needs of those learners.

For menus, mall ads, and grocery store flyers: Use colored sticky dots to cover the prices printed on menus and flyers. On the dots, round up prices to whole numbers that your students can recognize (numbers to 10, numbers to 20, numbers to 100 or higher). Use whole numbers only—no decimals.

For maps: Color code the cities or routes between cities.

For catalogs: Create "ad cards" using descriptions of real items cut from catalogs. Glue 1 item on each index card. Cover the actual price with a colored sticky dot. Round up the actual price to a whole number and write this new price on the dot.

For the money jar (or bag): Use a hot-glue gun to attach each coin to a separate 3 x 5-inch index card. Create 9 penny cards, 9 dime cards, 3 quarter cards, 9 nickel cards, and one $1 card. Place all the cards in the money bag. Although you can use plastic coins, real money is preferable.

Task Cards for Real-World Math

Directions

1. Select a task card.
2. Complete the activity.
3. Write the name of your task card and your answers in your math journal.

Mounds of Menu Choices

You'll need: 1 or more menus, money jar, pencil, math journal, calculator

Complete **1 or more** of the activities below. Write which number you chose and your answers in your math journal.

1. Choose a menu from your favorite restaurant. Write down your order from the menu. Total up the cost. Ask a friend to check your math. Pull enough money from the money jar to pay your bill. Again have a friend check. Does your friend agree that this is the right amount? If you don't agree, check your answer with a calculator.

2. Ask a friend to make up a math problem using different food combinations from a menu and different amounts of money you might have in your pocket to pay the bill. Each of you should figure out the answer separately, then you should compare answers. If you get different answers, use a calculator to check.

3. Make up a restaurant name and a menu for that restaurant. Work with a friend to decide on the meal you would order at the restaurant. What would be the cheapest meal for 2 people? The most expensive meal for 2 people? (Hint: You will need to choose 1 meal and double the cost.)

4. You and a friend split something at a restaurant. Choose a menu and decide together what you'd like to order from that menu. How much will you each pay if you each pay half of the total?

My Marvelous Math (3 Ms)

You'll need: Math journal, pencil, newspaper, magazine, menu, mail, or book

   In your math journal, explain what math you found today in one of the above resources. List 1 other resource and identify the math you find there as well. Then write a story problem with your marvelous math. Solve it or see if a friend can find the answer.

For Example:

Newspaper grocery coupon:
4 cans of tuna for $3
Soft tortillas: 10 for $1.00
12-pack of cola: $2.00

Paula went to the store and bought 30 tortillas. How much did she spend? $3.00

Maps Make Math Meaningful

You'll need: A map of your state, Unifix cubes, pencil, math journal

Complete **all** of these activities.

1. Decide where you would like to travel, starting from your city and going to another location in your state.
2. Connect a row of Unifix cubes between the 2 locations on the map. Make sure the Unifix cubes are snapped together.
3. Count the cubes.
4. Pretend that each Unifix cube shows a distance of 10 miles. Figure out how many miles long your trip would be.
5. Write in your journal:
    *   The name of the city or location you're traveling to
    *   How far away that location is from where you are now
    *   How long it would take you to get there if you went by car at 50 miles per hour
    *   How much it would cost you to fly to that location if the airline cost were $100 per 100 miles

Mall Madness

You'll need: An advertising flyer from a mall, pencil, math journal, calculator

Complete **all** of these activities.

1. Make a list of stores. Write down the items you would like to buy at each one.
2. Copy the chart on this card in your math journal.
3. Find 2 stores that have identical items. Compare the prices.
4. Calculate how much you will save by buying at the better price.
5. Ask a friend to find the answer separately, then compare answers. If you get different answers, use a calculator to double-check your work.

Item		
Store #1		
Store #2		
Cost difference		

Let's Eat!

You'll need: A grocery store flyer, pencil, math journal, calculator

Choose **1** of the problems on this card and solve it. Write the number you chose and your answer in your math journal.

1. Make a shopping list based on your favorite foods that are included on the flyer. Total up how much it will cost you to buy everything on your list.
2. Figure out what would be a good meal for your family, based on foods that are in the flyer. Make it a balanced meal (include a main course, a salad, fruit, bread, drinks, and a dessert). Figure out how much the meal would cost. Ask a friend to find the total separately, then compare your answers. If your answers don't agree, each of you should try again. If you still get different answers, ask another friend to try.
3. Your family is having a party. Each person in your family gets to invite 1 guest. Using the store flyer, decide what the menu will be for the party. How much will the food for the party cost? Ask a friend to find the total separately, then compare your answers. If your answers don't agree, use a calculator to double-check your work.
4. If your mom sent you to this store with $20, what could you buy to come closest to spending all your money?

Play-by-Play Sports

You'll need: The sports page from a newspaper for 1 or more days or weeks, pencil, math journal

Choose **1** of the problems on this card. Write the number you chose and your answer in your math journal.

1. Pick a team and see how many games they have lost or won since the season started. Then make a chart to compare your team's wins and losses. Write a math statement that shows how their number of wins or losses compares to their total number of games played so far. (For example: "The Bears have won 3 of their last 7 games. They have lost 2 of their last 7 games and tied 2 of their last 7 games.") Then make up a statement that predicts what you think will happen in the team's next game and why.

2. Pick a player to follow for the next 3 weeks. Use a chart to show how that player improves or falls below his own statistics for the next 3 weeks. Then make up a statement that predicts what you think will happen in the player's next game and why. (Example: "Joe Daring hit 3 homeruns in his first game this season. In the next game he scored 2 runs batted in. I think that in the next game he will probably help his team score at least 2 more runs.")

Wish List

You'll need: A gift catalog, shipping and handling chart, pencil, math journal

Create a wish list of things you would like to buy from the catalog, then complete **1** of these activities. Write the number you chose and your answer in your math journal.

1. Calculate what the cost would be if you bought all the items on your wish list. How much would shipping and handling add to the cost of your items?

2. If you earned $5 a week for an allowance and jobs around the house, how long would it take you to earn the money you would need to be able to buy the things on your wish list?

3. If you got $100 for your birthday instead of any presents from your friends, parents, and other people, what would you purchase? (Remember to include the cost of shipping and handling!)

Task Cards for Real-World Math

Directions

1. Select a task card.
2. Complete the activity.
3. Write the name of your task card and your answers in your math journal if the task card calls for that.

Mounds of Menu Choices 1

You'll need: 1 or more menus, pencil, math journal

Complete **all** of these steps.

1. Choose 2 items from the menu(s).
2. Draw the items in your journal.
3. Figure out how much these 2 items will cost all together.
4. Write the total cost in your journal.

Mounds of Menu Choices 2

You'll need: A menu, money jar

Complete **all** of these steps.

1. Looking at the menu, pick a snack to buy.
2. Take from the money jar the money you'll need.
3. Ask a friend to check that you've pulled out the right amount of money.
4. Return the money to the money jar.

Mounds of Menu Choices 3

You'll need: 1 or more menus, money jar

Complete **all** of these steps.

1. Looking at 1 or more menus, decide on an item you and a friend will share.
2. Take money from the jar to show the total cost.
3. Use "fair share" to divide the money equally between you and your friend. How much did you each pay?
4. Return the money to the money jar.

MOUNDS OF MENU CHOICES 4

You'll need: Menu, pencil, math journal

Write your answers to **all** of these questions in your math journal.

1. You have $4.00. Make a list of all the things you could buy from the menu.
2. How many different meals can you make with $4.00?
3. What 3 things could you buy and still get change?

MAPS MAKE MATH MEANINGFUL 1

You'll need: Map of your state, Unifix cubes, pencil, math journal

Complete **all** of these steps.

1. Find our city on the map.
2. Decide what city you want to travel to.
3. Lay Unifix cubes next to each other along the road between the 2 cities.
4. Each cube equals 100 miles. Count the cubes to find out how many miles away that city is and write the answer in your math journal. ("Houston to Galveston = ___ miles.")
5. Repeat for 5 other locations in the state.

MAPS MAKE MATH MEANINGFUL 2

You'll need: A map of your state, pencil, math journal

Complete **all** of these steps.

1. Look at your map and pick at least 5 cities or towns in our state.
2. List each of those towns or cities in your math journal.
3. Beside the name of each city, write how much it would cost to fly there if each mile cost $1. (For example, from Houston to Galveston is 100 miles, so it would cost $100.)

MALL MADNESS 1

You'll need: 2 ad cards, pencil, math journal

Complete **all** of these steps.

1. Choose 2 ad cards, each showing an item you would like to buy.
2. Compare the prices of the 2 items.
3. In your math journal, write a story to go with your 2 cards. (Example: "I went to Wal-Mart and found 2 things that I really wanted. One was a pencil case and cost $2. The other item was a gel pen set and cost $3. I decided to buy the pencil case because it was cheaper and I could use it for homework.")

Mall Madness 2

You'll need: 2 ad cards, pencil, math journal

Complete **all** of these activities and write the answers in your math journal.

1. Choose 2 ad cards that show items you would like to buy.
2. Add the prices of the items together to see how much they will cost. Ask a friend to check your answer. If you get different answers, both of you should add again. If you still get different answers, ask another friend to try.
3. If you have $5 in your piggy bank to spend, will that be enough? If not, how much more money do you need?

Let's Eat!!

You'll need: A store flyer, pencil, math journal, calculator

Choose **1** of the problems on this card. Solve the problem and write your answers in your math journal.

1. Choose 3 foods that you like to eat. Add up how much they will cost. Use a calculator to check yourself.
2. Find 3 foods your family likes. Add up the cost. Use a calculator to check yourself.
3. Your family is having a party. You need soda, chips, and cookies. Find these things in the flyer. Add up how much they will cost. Use a calculator to check yourself.
4. Mom sent you to the store with $10.00. Make a list of things you could buy without spending more than $10.00.

Play-by-Play Sports

You'll need: The sports page from your newspaper, pencil, math journal

In your math journal, write your answers to **both** of the questions on this card.

1. Find the report on your team's game. Did they win or lose?
2. What was the difference between the winning team's score and the losing team's score?

Wish List

You'll need: 3 to 5 ad cards, pencil, math journal, calculator

Choose **1** of the problems on this card. Solve the problem and write your answer in your math journal.

1. Choose 3 ad cards. Total the cost of the items on the cards. Use a calculator to check yourself.
2. Choose 4 ad cards. Total the cost of the items on the cards. Use a calculator to check yourself.
3. Choose 5 ad cards. Total the cost of the items on the cards. Use a calculator to check yourself.

Food Fun That Makes Learning Yummy!

Using food to engage your young learners makes counting, one-to-one correspondence, and math facts have real meaning. As students scoop, separate, build with, and measure food, they gain understanding of basic math concepts. Kinesthetic learners respond especially well to these activities. When you present math in terms of hands-on material that is familiar to the children, you instantly motivate them and get their attention. Here are some of my favorite ways to promote mathematical learning with food.

Cereal Proportions

PAIRS

Students work with cereal pieces to reinforce their understanding of terms like "greater than," "less than," "more," and "least."

MATERIALS

FOR EACH STUDENT

- 1 plastic condiment cup or a small ketchup container from a fast-food restaurant
- 1 copy of graph reproducible (page 132)
- Pencil
- Crayons

FOR THE CLASS

- 1 box of cereal that has different shapes and/or colors (Trix, Froot Loops, Lucky Charms, Alpha-Bits, or a seasonal cereal)

Directions

1. Give each child a cup and a copy of the reproducible.
2. Each child uses his cup to scoop out a serving of cereal.
3. He guesses how many cereal pieces are in his scoop and writes that guess at the top of his graph with a circle around it.
4. He pours out his cereal onto his graph and separates the cereal pieces by shape or color.
5. At the bottom of each graph section, the child draws a picture of 1 of the shapes or writes the name of 1 of the colors, being careful not to repeat any labels.
6. He places his cereal pieces in the appropriate sections of the graph, then marks on the graph the point where each column of cereal ends.
7. He removes all the cereal from his graph and puts it back in the cup.
8. He colors each section of the graph up to the line he marked.
9. He makes math statements (verbally or in writing below his graph) about his findings. Statements could include:
   I have more ___ than ___.   I have less ___ than ___.
   I have the same ___ and ___.   This section has the least.
   This section has the most.
10. After analyzing their cereal data, students can eat their cereal.

FOOD GRAPH

Yummy Swimmy

PAIRS

Use this activity to build estimation skills. To make it even more appealing, read Leo Lionni's story *Swimmy* to the class before handing out the crackers. Vary the size of the fish outline depending on the age of your students; the younger the students, the smaller the outline should be.

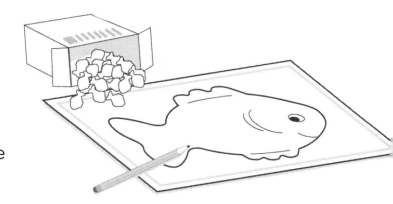

MATERIALS

FOR EACH STUDENT

- Outline of a fish shape (if you like, copy the reproducible on page 134)
- Goldfish crackers
- Pencil

Directions

1. Pair off students.
2. Hand out the outlines and give each student a pile of Goldfish crackers.
3. Each student estimates how many crackers it will take to fill her fish shape. (It's important to note that the first time your students do this, they're making guesstimates because they have no frame of reference.)
4. She writes that number above the fish shape within the circle.
5. She fills in the fish shape with crackers.
6. She counts the number of crackers it took to fill the shape and writes the actual number at the bottom of the paper. She compares the estimated number to the actual number.
7. Partners compare their results.

Repeat this activity later with fish outlines of different sizes. As a class, discuss how the students' estimates changed and why.

YUMMY SWIMMY

Fair Share

This is a good way to get students talking about sharing so that each has an equal amount. Introduce this activity by reading *The Very Grouchy Ladybug,* by Eric Carle.

MATERIALS

FOR EACH PAIR

- 2 plastic condiment cups (small ketchup containers from fast-food restaurants)
- Kix cereal
- 1 copy of "Fair Share" reproducible (page 136)

Directions

1. Pair off students.
2. Using a **condiment** cup, 1 child in each pair scoops out a portion of cereal.
3. Each partner guesses how many pieces are in the cup and writes his guess at the top of the reproducible, above the leaf.
4. Now it is "Fair Share" time!
5. The partners pour the cereal out of the cup and onto their reproducible.
6. Taking turns, each partner removes 1 piece of cereal at a time and places it in his cup.
7. Play continues until all the cereal is gone or only 1 piece remains, so it cannot be shared.
8. Each child counts the cereal pieces in his cup and writes that number on his side of the leaf.
9. Partners add their numbers together and then compare the total with their guesstimates.

_____'s guess: _____

_____'s guess: _____

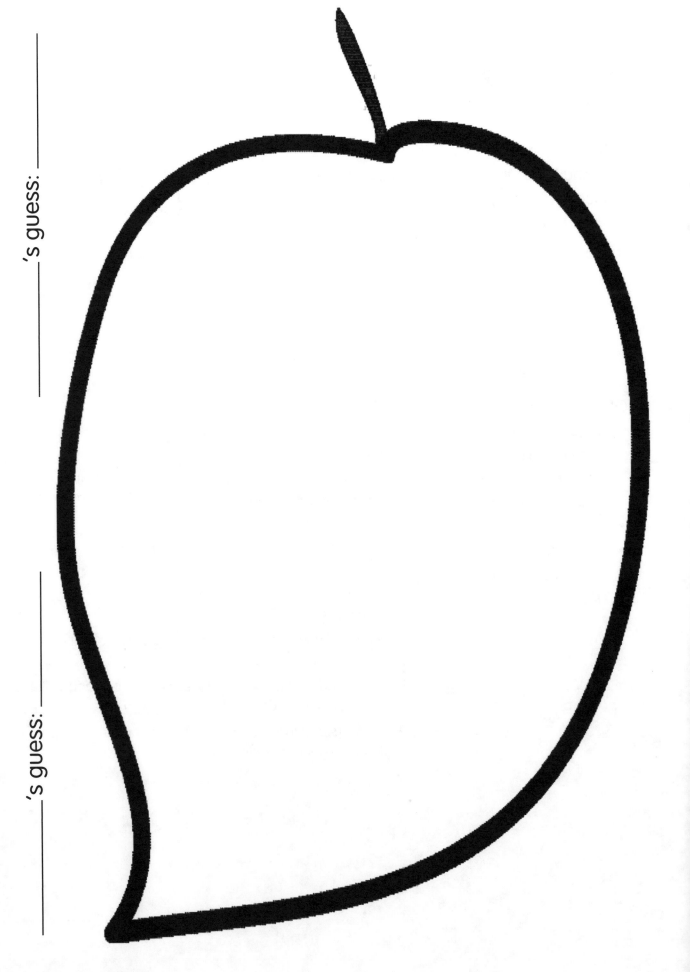

Cracker Graphs

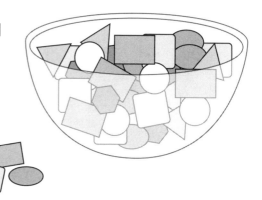

Here's a fun way for students to practice sorting and graphing.

MATERIALS

FOR THE CLASS
- Crackers in assorted shapes
- Bowl

FOR EACH STUDENT
- 1 plastic drink cup (4 ounces)
- 1 copy of the "Food Graph" reproducible (page 132)
- Marker

Directions

1. Pour the crackers into the bowl and mix them up.
2. Give each student a cup. This is her "portion cup."
3. Each child scoops out a portion of the crackers.
4. She pours the crackers out onto her copy of the reproducible and sorts the crackers by shape.
5. She then creates a graph to show how many crackers she has in each shape.

Cracker Creations

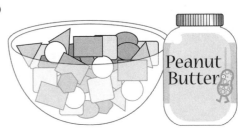

This one offers your construction learners a fun way to reinforce their understanding of shapes.

MATERIALS

FOR THE CLASS
- Crackers in assorted shapes
- Bowl
- Peanut butter or cream cheese

FOR EACH STUDENT
- 1 paper plate
- 1 plastic drink cup (4 ounces)
- Popsicle stick

Directions

1. Mix up the different crackers in the bowl.
2. Pair off students.
3. Give each student a paper plate, a cup to use as a scoop, some peanut butter or cream cheese to use as glue, and a Popsicle stick for spreading.
4. Each student uses his cup to measure out a portion of the crackers.
5. Working with the peanut butter or cream cheese to hold the pieces together, he builds a cracker creation.
6. When each student is finished, he describes to his partner what shapes are in his creation.

Follow My Directions

Like the previous activity, this one reinforces an understanding of shapes. It also builds listening and speaking skills.

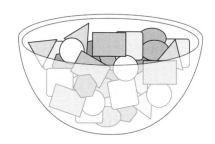

MATERIALS

FOR EACH STUDENT

- 1 paper plate
- Popsicle stick

FOR THE CLASS

- Crackers in assorted shapes
- Peanut butter or cream cheese

Directions

1. Pair off students.
2. Give each student a paper plate, a Popsicle stick for spreading, a small pile of crackers, and some peanut butter or cream cheese.
3. Partners sit back to back, each with her "building materials" in front of her.
4. One child builds a cracker creation.
5. As she puts her materials together, she tells her partner exactly what she's doing.
6. The partner attempts to build the same creation, using the same shapes, without looking at what the original builder is doing.
7. Both move away from their creations, and they compare results.
8. The partners swap roles and repeat the process.

The Long & Short of It

Students love learning about measurement with these sweet "snakes." And mixing the dough with their hands isn't exactly a hardship!

MATERIALS

FOR EACH STUDENT

- Edible Fun Dough (see recipe)
- 1 clean tray
- Adding machine tape
- Froot Loops
- Pencil

FOR THE TEACHER

- 1/2 cup measuring cup

Directions

1. Make a batch of Edible Fun Dough. Give each student approximately 1/2 cup of dough.
2. On her tray, each student rolls her Edible Fun Dough into a snake shape.
3. She tears off a piece of adding machine tape the same length as her snake.
4. She measures the length of her snake by lining up Froot Loops along the strip, making sure the cereal pieces are touching, and then counts the Froot Loops.
5. She writes the Froot Loops count on the adding machine tape, along with her name.
6. At the end of the day, students make comparison statements about the snakes. They might say something like:
   - My snake is longer than Caroline's by_____ Froot Loops.
   - My snake is shorter than Sabiana's by_____ Froot Loops.
   - My snake is the same length as Jacob's.

Variation

Use pennies instead of Froot Loops to determine how much each snake is "worth."

Edible Fun Dough

1 can (16 ounces) ready-made frosting

1 1/2 cups confectioners' sugar

1 cup peanut butter or cream cheese

Mix all the ingredients together to form a workable dough.

DATA WAY WITH GRAPHS & GLYPHS

Graphs and glyphs can help young children to understand and analyze mathematical relationships by presenting those relationships in a simple, visual way.

Glyphs help students make the connection between real-world data—especially data about themselves and their world—and visual representations. Graphs help to make that same connection, with the added element of quantity. When a student creates and explains a graph that shows 10 classmates prefer chocolate ice cream and 5 prefer vanilla, that student sees and internalizes the fact that more prefer chocolate. He sees the relationship between the numbers.

Graphs and glyphs are a great example of how differentiation works so beautifully with math. You can begin with whole-class instruction, allow students to explore and practice in small groups and independently, and then come back together to share learning. You can also use a variety of formats to appeal to all types of learners. This is where differentiation can make such a difference!

If your students are going to experience the true impact of graphs, then graphs should be a weekly or even daily experience. Subjects for graphs can be your attendance, milk or lunch count, or number of bus riders vs. car riders vs. walkers. You'll think of many topics for charts that communicate real numbers and are directly related to things your students are interested in.

To introduce these ways of working with data in your differentiated classroom, I've developed something I call "Training Camp for Graphs and Glyphs." The following pages explain how it works.

Training Camp for Graphs & Glyphs

MATERIALS

- Camera
- Cardstock cut into 2-inch squares
- Magnet squares
- Glue
- 22 x 28-inch sheet of craft paper
- Permanent marker
- Quart-sized resealable plastic bag
- Copies of reproducible (page 145)
- Sticky notes

Preparing for Training Camp

The basis of training camp is a graph on which each student will indicate his response every day. To prepare for that, you need to set up the student response cards and the graph itself ahead of time. Let's start with the response cards.

1. Take a picture of each student and glue the photo onto a 2 x 2-inch piece of cardstock. Laminate.
2. Glue a magnet square to the back.

Next, with the cards ready, you can move on to setting up the student response board.

1. With the marker, divide the craft paper in half vertically, with each half measuring 11 x 28 inches.
2. Flip the paper over. On the other side, divide the paper vertically again, but this time, divide it in thirds.
3. Laminate the craft paper.
4. Attach the chart to the side of a metal file cabinet or magnetic whiteboard.
5. Store the response cards in a large resealable plastic bag. Tape the bag next to the chart.

Now you're ready to begin training your students to enter their responses on the class graph each morning.

Training Camp Begins

For the first month of school, write the "question of the day" on a sentence strip each day and tape the strip above your blank graph. Start with simple 2-choice charts: "Are you a boy or a girl?" "Do you like pizza—yes or no?" "Do you like to play inside or outside?" "Would you rather be read to or read to yourself?" As part of your morning routine, have each child go to the chart and place his response card in the appropriate column. Explain that the response

Are You a Boy or a Girl?
BOY   GIRL

card should always be placed in the first available spot in that column—no blank spaces allowed!

When you process the chart with the class, have the students talk about the number of responses in each category—always comparing each part to the total number. "There are 12 girls out of 25 students and 13 boys out of 25 students in our class." Part to whole is an important element in data analysis.

You'll also want to ask more questions about the data each graph is showing. Your objective is to get students thinking about the relationships among the numbers. To do that, try asking questions like these:

- Which column has the most? How many more?
- Which has the least? How many fewer?
- Which choice has zero responses?
- Which choices have the same number?
- Are there more ___ or more ___?
- Are there fewer ___ or fewer ___?
- What other information can we get from this graph?
- How could we change the question for next time? What do you predict will be our responses?

Students can respond to these questions orally. They can also write in their mini math lab books (see pages 181–83) about what they've done or what they've noticed. If you're working with younger children, you can use an anchor chart and record the class's responses yourself.

Building on Training Camp

As the year goes on, continue using the question of the day, but gradually build up to greater numbers of choices: "Which animal do you like the most: cat, dog, or bird?" "When were you born: fall, winter, spring, or summer?"

Variations on the Training Camp Graph

- If you prefer, you can use poster board rather than craft paper and substitute pieces of Velcro for the magnets. Attach 1 part of the Velcro to the back of the student response cards and glue the other part of the Velcro in columns on both sides of the chart. You will need more squares of Velcro on the chart than you have pictures.

- With younger students, you may want to add picture clues to the question of the day.

- As you work your way up to graphs with more variables, you'll need to create additional graphs with more columns.

Graphing Independently

In "training camp," you provided the choices. Now ask your students to come up with some questions for their friends to respond to. They can build on what they've learned, this time collecting data from friends and family to create their own graphs.

You might give them copies of the "Pet Survey" reproducible on page 145 to get them started with their data collection. Explain that each child is to complete a separate graph, based on information he gets from friends and neighbors.

Once the students have completed their individual graphs, you can consolidate this information into a single class graph. Have each student put his name on a sticky note. He should then determine which type of pet was the most popular in his survey and put the sticky note with his name on it in the appropriate column of the class graph. Together the class can look at the overall trends regarding which pet is most popular. Remove those sticky notes and create a new graph in the same way, this time reporting which pet was the *least* popular, or not chosen at all.

Next, ask students to come up with some questions of their own and to gather responses from friends and family (or from others as appropriate). They can create surveys having to do with favorite foods, restaurants, TV shows, video games, the number of people in a family, etc. If you like, use the reproducible from the "Pet Survey" and just change the category headings.

Then, to engage even more students, allow them to explore data in a range of other ways with the activities on pages 146–51.

PET SURVEY

Directions
1. Ask your friends and neighbors what pets they have.
2. Color in the graph below to show the results of your survey. Use a different color for each category.
3. Be ready to share your results with the class and compare what you and your friends found.

	dog	cat	fish	gerbil	other
11					
10					
9					
8					
7					
6					
5					
4					
3					
2					
1					

Graphing in Three Dimensions

MATERIALS

- Shower curtain
- Masking tape or permanent marker
- Index cards
- Items for graphing
- Butcher paper
- Construction paper
- Scissors
- Tape
- Plastic plates

Novelty and variety engage children, and graphing in different formats appeals to kinesthetic learners in particular. Looking at numbers in many different ways reinforces students' understanding of number relationships, too.

A Floor Graph

This is ideal for graphing with concrete objects such as apples or valentines. To make one, start with an inexpensive shower curtain. It needs to be a solid color; any pattern will distract from the graph. Spread the curtain on the floor and mark off grid lines with masking tape or a colored permanent marker so that you have roughly 6 columns of 6 rectangles each. (Tip: If you have a large tiled floor, lay the shower curtain over the tiles and trace along the lines to make your grid.) If you don't need all 6 columns for a particular graph, you can fold under the extra columns. If you need more than 6 columns, use construction paper to extend the graphing space. Create a category card as a header for each column, and you're ready to start graphing.

If you're graphing apples, your category cards might say, "red," "yellow," and "green." You would have each student bring in her favorite type of apple and place it in the appropriate column.

If you're graphing valentines, use an assortment of valentine cards and have students sort them into categories. Your category cards could be "TV show characters," "animals," and "movie characters," or whatever else is appropriate for the collection you have. Magazine pictures of food could be grouped as shown in the illustration. Or you can make this a very open-ended activity by letting the students determine the categories.

A Bar Graph

Here's another way to add variety to your graphing lessons. Draw the appropriate number of horizontal rows on butcher paper, post the paper on the wall, and ask the students to complete the graph. Suppose the question of the day is, "Are you a boy or a girl?" You would cut out construction paper outlines of boy shapes and girl shapes and give those to the students. Have each child tape his cutout to the bar graph in the appropriate section, making sure the cutouts are lined up so that students can see which section is longer. Then lead students in comparing the data, posing questions similar to those you asked with earlier graphs.

Converting a Bar Graph to a Circle Graph

This activity is a great lesson in number relationships. Let's say you're still working with that graph of boys and girls. Remove all the cutouts from the girl section of the bar graph and tape them together so it looks like the "girls" are holding hands. Now remove the cutouts from the boy section of the graph. Tape those together so it looks like the "boys" are holding hands. Connect the girl section to the boy section so that they're all holding hands in a circle. You have just turned a bar graph into a circle graph!

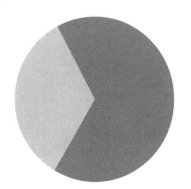
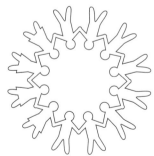

Place your circle of cutouts on a large piece of butcher paper or a solid-color shower curtain. Now you need to create the sections of the circle graph. To do this, find the center of the circle and draw a line from that point to 1 of the points where "boy meets girl" in the cutouts. Draw a second line, this time from the center to the *other* point where the cutouts meet. Draw in the outline of the circle on the butcher paper, then remove your cutouts and have the students color in the pie sections.

A Paper-Plate Pie Chart

Want to do more? As long as your graph has only 2 sets of data, you can illustrate it in another way. You'll need 2 disposable plastic plates, each a different color. Take the first plate and make a cut from the edge to the center. Repeat with the second plate. Slide the 2 cut plates together so that both colors show, then rotate the plates to match the pie slices in the butcher paper circle graph.

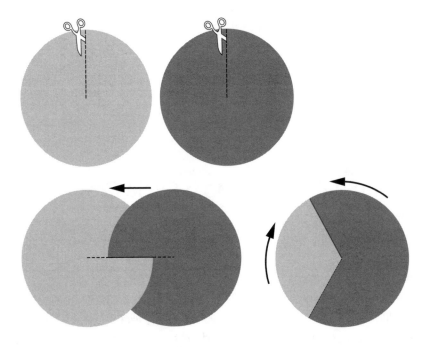

Water Preferences

MATERIALS

- Marker
- Paper
- Tape
- 2 identical clear plastic containers (each 1 quart or larger)
- Water
- Water bucket
- Small plastic cup

Preparation

Create 1 label for each of a pair of survey statements related to water. Tape 1 of the statements to each container. Possible statements include:

"I like swimming in a pool better." Or, "I like swimming in a lake better."

"I took swimming lessons last summer." Or, "I did not take swimming lessons last summer."

"I was on a swim team last summer." Or, "I was not on a swim team last summer."

Procedure

Each child fills a cup with water from the bucket and places the water in the container with the label that best describes his water experience. The height of the water in each container tells the math story. Have students write independently in their math journals about what they observe from the data, or ask them to buddy up and compare responses.

DVD Darlings

MATERIALS

- Tape
- Cases from 3 or 4 DVDs your students enjoy watching
- 2 pieces of poster board
- Scissors
- Marker
- Clothespins

Preparation

Tape the DVD cases across the top of 1 sheet of poster board. Cut the other sheet of poster board into 1-inch-wide strips (1 for each DVD), saving the leftover poster board for another project. Tape the strips so that 1 hangs down from each DVD. Write each child's name on a clothespin.

Procedure

Hand out the clothespins. Each child places his clothespin on the strip under the DVD he enjoys watching the most.

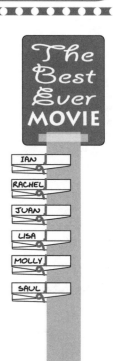

Birthday Bash

MATERIALS

FOR THE CLASS
- Card stock
- Markers

FOR EACH STUDENT
- 1 birthday candle
- Play Doh

Preparation

Write the name of a different month on each of 12 cards. Fold the cards tent-style so they stand up. Line up the cards on a table.

Procedure

Give each child a candle and a small ball of Play Doh. Explain that she is to mold the Play Doh around the base of her candle to make the candle stand up, then place the candle in front of the card for her birthday month. Encourage students to place their candles in a straight line coming down from the month card so the class can compare the numbers of candles for the different months.

Soup-er Spoons

MATERIALS

FOR THE CLASS

- Shower curtain floor graph (see page 146)
- 3 to 4 unopened cans of soup

FOR THE TEACHER

- Permanent marker

FOR EACH STUDENT

- 1 plastic spoon

Preparation

Set up your shower curtain grid on the floor. Place the cans just off the grid, either to the left or at the top, with 1 can to a row or column. Use the marker to write the name of each student on a plastic spoon.

Procedure

Hand out the spoons. Each child places her spoon in a section of the grid that corresponds to her favorite soup. Explain that it's important to place each spoon in the next available grid space for that student's choice; empty spaces will spoil the effect.

Have students write independently in their math journals about what they observe from the data, or ask them to buddy up and compare responses.

Note: This can also be done with cereal boxes, frozen dinner or frozen pizza boxes, ice-cream cartons, yogurt containers, and so on.

Introducing Glyphs

MATERIALS

FOR EACH STUDENT

- Construction paper
- Pencils
- Scissors
- Glue

FOR THE CLASS

- Construction paper
- Shower curtain graph (see page 146)
- Markers

A glyph is a form of picture writing that conveys information. "Glyphs" is short for hieroglyphics. Making glyphs requires students to assemble data, to represent that data graphically, and to interpret the graphic representations of their classmates. These are all important skills for budding mathematicians to learn.

Besides, glyphs are fun! When you work with glyphs in the classroom, each child creates a glyph with elements that represent specific information about that child. The individual features of the finished glyph tell a story about the person who created it.

The first step in working with a glyph is to decide on the legend. Print the legend on a 12 x 18-inch sheet of construction paper. Place the legend on the center of the bulletin board where you are going to display the children's individual glyphs. The legend should include the basic shape, the color, the pattern, any special decorations, and so on. Each child is going to create a glyph that shows something about herself, based on the legend.

Let's say your students are creating apple glyphs.

1. Make an enlarged copy of the reproducible legend on page 155 as a reference. Cut sheets of red, green, and brown construction paper in fourths.

2. Provide students with the pieces of construction paper. Make sure they have pencils, scissors, and glue.

3. Have each child draw and cut out an apple. Following the legend, each girl should make a green apple and each boy should make a red apple.

4. Each left-handed child should draw and cut out a stem, then glue it into place so it's pointed to the left; each right-handed child should do the same but make the stem point to the right.

5. Now, each child adds 1 leaf for each person who lives in her house.

6. Any student who has a library card adds a worm to his apple. So a green apple with a left-pointing stem, 3 leaves, and a worm is the glyph made by a left-handed girl who lives in a household of 3 people (including herself) and has a library card.

7. Post the legend and the student glyphs on the bulletin board.

Connecting Glyphs & Graphs

One of the best things about glyphs is that they feed so beautifully into graphing. Each attribute of a glyph gives you data for a shower curtain graph that you can create with your students. When you talk about each attribute with your students, simply remove the glyphs from the board and lay them on your shower curtain graph as you talk about the numbers represented. In the case of the apple glyphs, for example, you might start with 1 column of green apples and 1 column of red apples to compare the numbers of boys and girls in the class. This helps students to make those real-world connections that are so important.

More Work with Glyphs

As a next step in working with glyphs, create glyphs with another theme the students can relate to (see box for ideas). Print a copy of the legend on a 12 x 18-inch sheet of construction paper. Model how to work with the legends to create the glyphs. Then set students loose to create their own individualized versions, following the legend. Later you and your students can create other glyphs according to units of study and time of year, but if you start with ones that are highly personalized, you'll get your students' interest.

Once students understand how glyphs work, you can set up your current glyph project as a center with construction paper, scissors, glue and markers. After students construct their glyphs, have them place the glyphs on the bulletin board. Be sure to post the appropriate legend next to each group of glyphs. Children love to display their glyphs and have parents guess which child belongs to which glyph.

More Ideas for Glyphs

Build on what your students have done so far with glyphs. Use a basic shape that reflects the time of year (gift packages in December, snow people in January, hearts in February) or a current unit of study (Pilgrims, geometric shapes). Then continue that theme with colors and decorations that make each glyph unique. Ask students to create glyphs that represent attributes like these:

- Number of letters in your first name (2 to 4, 5 to 7, 8 or more)
- Preferences, or "I'd rather have . . ." (hot dog, hamburger, or grilled cheese)
- Things I have (pets, sports equipment, collections)
- Things I've done (swum in a lake or a pool or a creek)
- Personal facts (brothers, sisters, only child)

Using Glyphs Across the Curriculum

To create a glyph based on a unit of study, first determine what basic shape you can use to represent the unit. For example, if you were studying Columbus, you could use an outline of the base of a sailing ship (without the sails). A student who is a boy would add 1 mast; a girl would add 2 masts. The shape of the sails would be the shape of the continent where the student was born; a student who was born in China would add a sail shaped like an outline of Asia. Each student could create a banner to fly off the mast, with the color of the banner representing (based on a legend you provide) the continent the student would like to explore. The student could even put stripes on the banner to represent the number of years she has lived in the United States.

In this case, you might provide a legend like this one:

Number of masts: boy = 1, girl = 2

Shape of sail: continent where you were born

Color of banner: continent you would like to explore
(Europe = green, Australia = red, Africa = orange, Asia = yellow, North America = blue, South America = purple, Antarctica = white)

Stripes on banner: number of years you have lived in the United States

APPLE GLYPH

Apple color:	Green = girl Red = boy
Stem:	Pointed right = right-handed Pointed left = left-handed
Leaves:	Add 1 leaf to the stem for every person living in your house.
Worm:	Add a worm if you have a library card.

PHYSICAL GAMES THAT TEACH MATH CONCEPTS

T hese activities are especially good choices for the bodily-kinesthetic child, because physical games give these students the opportunity to manipulate and move as they work with math. But don't limit their use to your kinesthetic learners. Virtually all children are quickly engaged by anything you can describe as a game!

Eggs-ceptional Fun

PLAYERS: 1

Concept: Number fluency

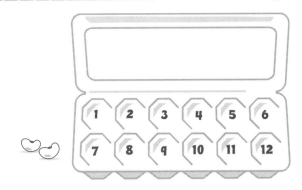

MATERIALS

- Empty egg carton with the sections numbered 1 through 12
- 2 small items
- 1 mini math lab book

To Play

1. The student places the items in the carton and then closes and shakes the carton.
2. She opens the carton and notes the numbers of the sections where her items have landed.
3. She adds these 2 numbers together and records the equation in her mini math lab book.
4. She repeats the process 5 more times.

Variation

Instead of adding the numbers, the student subtracts 1 from the other.

Money Bags

Concepts: Measurement, money values, computation

MATERIALS

FOR EACH STUDENT
- 2 Styrofoam coffee cups
- 1 penny

FOR THE ROBBER
- 1 "money bag" (or other type of container)

To Play

1. All children sit in a circle.
2. One child is designated as the "robber." Everyone except the robber receives a penny and 2 cups.
3. The robber gets the money bag and turns his back to the group.
4. Each child places both her cups in front of her and puts a coin under 1 of them.
5. When ready, the children put their hands behind their backs. The group calls, "Put and take!" to let the robber know that they're ready to play.
6. The robber stands in front of the first child to his left. He points to 1 of the cups and asks, "Is the penny under there?"
7. The child turns over the cup indicated and answers either, "Yes, the penny is there" or "No, the penny is not there."
8. If the robber was correct, he collects the coin and puts it in his money bag, then repeats the process with the next child.
9. After he's visited all the children, the robber counts his "take."
10. The robber returns to his original place and the next child in the circle becomes the robber.

Variations

1. Instead of pennies, use nickels, dimes, or quarters.
2. Use mixed coins and have the robber count the value of the dimes, then add on the value of the nickels, and finally add on the value of the pennies to see how much his loot is worth.

Note

Before playing this game, you may want to share with students your favorite book about money. Two of my particular favorites are *Pigs Will Be Pigs*, by Amy Axelrod, and *Alexander, Who Used to Be Rich Last Sunday*, by Judith Viorst.

Walk-On Math

PLAYERS: 2

Concept: Number fluency

MATERIALS

- 13 clear transparencies (8 1/2 x 11 inches)
- Scissors
- Clear shower curtain liner
- Clear mailing tape
- 25 unlined index cards (5 x 8 inches)
- 2 lightweight plain paper plates (9 inches)
- Large paper clip
- Ruler
- Marker
- Pencil

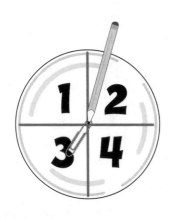

To Prepare the Game Board

1. The goal is to create pockets on the shower curtain liner.
2. Cut each transparency into 2 pieces, each 5 1/2 x 8 1/2 inches.
3. Place the shower curtain liner on the floor.
4. Space the transparency pieces evenly across and down the shower curtain liner, creating 5 rows with 5 pieces in each row. Discard the extra piece.
5. Use the clear mailing tape to secure the pieces to the shower curtain liner on the sides and bottom of each piece, leaving the top of the piece open.
6. Number the index cards from 1 through 25.
7. Insert a numbered index card into each pocket, being careful to keep the cards in sequence. You want the numbers to show through the untaped side of the shower curtain.

To Create Game Spinners

1. With a ruler and a marker, divide 1 of the paper plates in half. Write a plus sign on 1 half and a minus sign on the other half. This is the function spinner.
2. Divide the other plate into fourths. Number each section from 1 through 4. This is the number spinner.

To Play

1. Lay the curtain on the floor so that the pockets are on the bottom.
2. The first player stands on the "1."
3. The partner places the tip of a pencil through the paper clip in the center of the number spinner. While holding the pencil stationary, he spins the paper clip around the pencil to determine the number of spaces to be moved.
4. The partner then spins the function spinner to determine whether the player needs to move forward or backward.

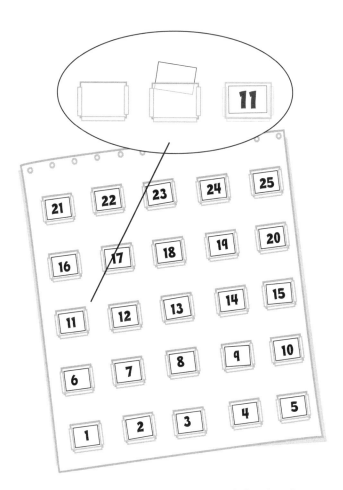

5. The player moves the number of spaces determined by the number spinner. If a student is standing on "1" and the partner spins a "2" and a "+," the student must move and count 2 spaces to get to the "3" space. If following the directions from the number spinner and the function spinner would result in a negative number (for example, the student is standing on 1 and the partner spins a minus and a 2), the player loses his turn.

6. The player's turn ends when he reaches "25." (He doesn't have to land on that exact number. If he's on "24" and the partner spins "3," he's still completed his turn.)

7. The other student takes her turn and repeats the process.

Variations

1. Make this game more challenging by dividing the number spinner into eighths and numbering the sections from 1 through 8.

2. For number recognition and counting on, use number cards as above, but work with the number spinner only. The child moves the number of spaces indicated by the spinner and must be able to accurately identify the new number that he's standing on.

3. For skip counting, make cards that increase by 2s, 5s, or 10s. Work only with the number spinner with the 4 sections. The child starts with the number he's standing on and moves ahead by skip counting. For instance, if the child is standing on "15," the cards increase by 5s, and you spin a "3," the child must skip count ahead, saying, "20, 25, 30," and moving to the "30" block.

4. For instant number recognition, make cards with dot patterns (like those on a domino) from 1 through 12. Because you have 25 pockets and 12 patterns, you'll have more than 1 card for some patterns. Place the cards randomly on the curtain, not in numerical order. Use only the number spinner. The child moves ahead the number of spaces indicated and must accurately identify the new dot pattern on which she's standing.

Disk Spin

Concepts: Adding/subtracting, number fluency

MATERIALS

- CD-ROM disk (can be a demo disk)
- Permanent marker or paint pen
- 1-inch washer from a rubber garden hose
- Hot-glue gun
- Glue sticks
- 2 or more index cards, each 5 x 8 inches
- Calculator
- Mini math lab book
- Game marker (penny, washer, bean, etc.)

To Prepare the Spinner

1. With the permanent marker or paint pen, divide the disk into 8 equal segments. Number the segments 1 through 8.
2. On the back of the CD, hot-glue the washer into place around the hole.
3. Draw an arrow at the top of the 5-inch side of 1 of the index cards. This is the spinner card.

To Prepare the Game Cards

1. Mark off each card in 1-inch squares.
2. In each square, write either "add" or "subtract." Underneath each word write a number from 0 through 12.

To Play

1. The child starts at the square in the top left corner. Using the current day of the month, the child follows the directions for that space (either adding or subtracting the given number). If he's playing on November 10 and the first square says, "Add 2," his equation would be "10 + 2 = 12." He checks with a calculator and writes his equation in his mini math lab book.
2. The child places the computer disk on the spinner card, places the tip of a pencil inside the hole of the disk, and spins.
3. He moves the game marker the number of spaces indicated on the spinner.
4. He combines the answer from the previous equation with the label in the new square to create a new equation. So if the answer to the first problem was 12 and he landed on a square marked "Subtract 3," his equation would be "12 – 3 = 9."
5. He writes the new equation in his mini math lab book.
6. He continues down the game board, working left to right across each row until he reaches the bottom of the board.

One or Two— It's Up to You

Concepts: Logic, reasoning

MATERIALS

- 12 identical items (coins, rocks, cubes, and so on) on a tray

To Play

1. Either person may begin the game. The first player takes either 1 item or 2 items (his choice) from the tray.

2. The second player takes either 1 item or 2 items (she doesn't have to take the same number as her opponent).

3. Play continues in the same way until only 1 object is left. The person picking up the last item wins.

4. After the game has been played several times, ask your students if they have developed a strategy for winning. If they have, ask them to explain it to the class.

Variations

1. Change the number of items on the tray or allow students to take up to 3 items in each turn; challenge them to see if that affects the outcome of the game.

2. Change the rules by declaring that the person who takes the last object is the one who *loses* the game.

Domino Do-Dads

Concept: Number fluency

MATERIALS

- Set of dominoes
- 1 mini math lab book

To Play

1. The student lays all the dominoes face down on the table and then turns over 2 dominoes.

2. The student adds the number of dots on the top section of each domino to the number of dots on the bottom section of that same domino.

3. In his mini math lab book, he draws and writes the answer to the question, "Which domino had more dots, or were they the same?"

4. Using the dot totals he's just calculated, the student subtracts the smaller number of dots from the larger number.

5. He records the results in his mini math lab book.

Variation

The student turns over 2 dominoes and calculates the total number of dots of the 2 combined. Then he adds the number of dots on *each* domino. Finally, he subtracts the smaller number from the larger number on each.

Planning & Assessment Tools

The Differentiated Unit Lesson Plan

As you fill in the following checklist, pick and choose those activities that will fit your class curriculum and the content specifics for your particular unit of study. Keep copies of these checklists and refer back to them when planning future lessons to ensure you are including the variety and novelty that will energize your teaching and your students' learning. Modify your lesson plans and your math lab options to address the unique learners that you have in your classroom. This is the basis for a differentiated math class.

Explanation of Terms

The "Unit Lesson Plan Checklist" is a tool for implementing the strategies presented in this book and adapting them to the needs of your students. Here's a quick guide to the pieces it includes.

1. STANDARDS

As has often been said, you must "begin with the end in mind." This requires that you as the teacher clearly identify the standard you're addressing and have a strong sense of what "enduring understandings" your students will need to master as they work to meet that standard. The next step is to build the basic math skills that will support those understandings.

2. PRE-ASSESSMENT

Before beginning to teach a unit, you need to assess your students. Pre-assessment is critical for good teaching.

Readiness

What students have what skills already under control? Who needs more support to get the essentials down? Who is ready for more challenging material and in what areas?

To determine these things, you need to assess where your students are in their basic math facts and understandings. Some teacher guides or districts provide a formal pre-assessment test that can be used to identify your students' readiness for a particular unit of study. Other pre-assessment forms can be found on pages 175–78. However, pre-assessment does not necessarily have to be a formal process. Information from students' journals and portfolios can provide a window into student thinking, and you can also pre-assess with anecdotal information (your observations during energizers, free exploration, game time, individual instruction, and so on).

Learning modalities (learning styles and multiple intelligences)

You need to assess how each student learns and then structure your lesson to accommodate different learning styles and intelligences. Is this child a tactile-kinesthetic learner? Does he need to move around? Does she need to see it or talk about it? Examining the similarities between musical notes and fractions may interest the musical child. Learning how to add and subtract using measuring may attract the construction learner. Use the reproducibles on pages 171 and 173 to assess each of your students.

Some students prefer to work with other students. Providing opportunities for paired and small-group discussions works well for these children. Other students prefer to work on their own at their own pace. It's a good idea to ask students often how they enjoy working in your classroom. Then you can plan activities together that take into consideration how they can best learn and communicate their learning of the material.

Interests

What are each student's interests outside of the classroom? See page 172. The outside world holds a lot of problem-solving opportunities for math. Is this child interested in racing cars? Sports statistics? Does she like to shop? Children who have used their own money to purchase items often enjoy using coins and figuring out the value of currency.

3. CONTENT

What do you want the students to learn? While planning your unit, you need to determine:

- **Concepts** that you are going to be teaching
- **Vocabulary** that is involved with the concepts
- **Skills** necessary to master the concepts
- **Facts** basic to understanding the concepts

4. PROCESS

The process of how you will teach the concepts and how the students will learn them becomes part of the planning.

Establish prior knowledge

What do your students know about the real-world applications of this math concept? How will you find that out?

Focus activities

Make sure that the planned activities are varied and use higher-level thinking such as analysis, synthesis, and evaluation.

Flexible grouping

An important part of the process is ensuring that your groupings change as activities change. Are you consistently assigning the same children to the same ability groups time after time? Consider heterogeneous groupings or groups organized by interests or learning modalities. Or seek out areas in which different students excel, so groupings change often and students don't feel labeled as being always in a certain group.

5. PRODUCT

How will students show what they've learned?

6. ONGOING ASSESSMENT AND ADJUSTMENT

Critical to the success of a differentiated classroom is ongoing assessment to ensure that the "leapers" in your class (those who make quick progress at any level of their learning) and the "slow thinkers" (those who take a more leisurely approach but can still arrive at the same destination) are all progressing toward the essential understandings of your topic.

UNIT LESSON PLAN CHECKLIST

1. **Standards.** What is the basic math concept or topic?

   Essential question(s):

   Student should know:

   Student should be able to do:

2. **Pre-assessment.** What means will you use to pre-assess your students?

Readiness	**Learning modalities**	**Interests**
___ learning logs	___ checklists	___ checklists
___ checklists	___ observations	___ observations
___ journals		___ journals
___ observations		___ portfolios
___ portfolios		
___ rubrics		

3. **Content.** What do the students need to learn?

   Concepts

   Vocabulary

   Skills

   Facts

4. **Process.** What approaches will you use to engage your students?

Establish prior knowledge	**Focus activities**	**Flexible grouping**
___ quiz	___ energizers	___ large group
___ survey	___ free exploration	___ small group
___ KWL chart	___ games	___ pairs
___ journal	___ related literature	___ individuals
___ brainstorm	___ calendar activities	___ heterogeneous
___ interactive Web site(s)	___ songs/rhymes	___ homogeneous
	___ anchor activities	___ random
	___ teacher modeling	
	___ guest speaker	

5. **Product.** How can they show what they know?

___ journals
___ mini math lab books
___ Choice Option Menu
___ projects
___ explorations
___ graphic organizers
___ portfolios
___ surveys
___ math stories
___ math songs
___ word problems
___ math posters
___ graphs
___ glyphs
___ book connections
___ interactive Web sites
___ task cards

6. **Ongoing assessment and adjustment**. How will students demonstrate an understanding of the concept?

___ quiz
___ performance
___ products
___ presentations
___ demonstrations
___ learning logs
___ checklist
___ rubric
___ portfolios
___ unit test

The Differentiated Daily Lesson Plan

Now that you have an outline of your unit of study based on the "Unit Lesson Plan Checklist," you can use the following template to plan your daily math lessons. Be as creative as you need to be to address the needs of your students. Remember, variety builds enthusiastic problem solvers!

One of the best things about a differentiated math program is that it's so flexible. There are 3 basic parts to this approach: direct instruction, exploration and guided practice, and sharing; the length of time you devote to each of those pieces each day is up to you.

One approach is to follow the basic timeframe outlined below, including all 3 pieces every day.

A second is to use the math lab just once a week, on Friday, to give students a chance to review and practice the concepts you've presented earlier in the week. (Your direct instruction time that day would probably be shorter.)

A third approach is to allow a full 75-minute time slot for math on Monday, and to use that time for direct instruction and setting the tasks for the week. Tuesday through Friday you would use shorter blocks of time to focus on exploration and guided practice and on sharing. If it works better for your class, you can even save the sharing component for a different time, maybe at the end of the day or the first part of the next day.

Let's take a look at how the pieces of the math lab approach can work together. Decisions on how much time to allow for each piece are unique to each situation. They depend on the time you have available, the needs of your students, and the purpose of the lesson. Keep in mind that flexibility is a key part of differentiation.

Section 1—
Direct Instruction (up to 30 minutes)

This is your opportunity to focus your students' attention through energizers, introduce a new concept to the whole group, or reinforce a concept you're already working on. It's also the time to give directions for the exploration and guided practice phase. Look at your "Unit Lesson Plan Checklist" for ideas.

During direct instruction, you have a chance to model your thinking just as you do in the reading classroom. You might demonstrate a real-life use of math by using a grocery store advertising flyer to plan the week's shopping, showing students how you make a list with prices (rounding up the numbers) and estimating what the bill will be. This prepares them to then try similar activities on their own (in this example, working with the task cards on pages 122 and 128).

Section 2— Exploration & Guided Practice (up to 60 minutes)

During this time, students at different levels might solve problems or work from a menu of choices to select other ways of practicing their skills. Some students might be in small groups, completing a multileveled lesson structured by you, while others might be working on individualized or paired explorations.

Take this opportunity to clipboard cruise (walk around the room with a clipboard), making observations and recording anecdotal notes of conversations that need to be shared. This can be a good time to conference with individual students, to evaluate others individually or in small groups, and to reteach any material for which students have weak or incorrect understandings. As a means of cementing new learning, encourage students to dialogue with each other about their thinking, too.

Section 3— Sharing (10 to 15 minutes)

Bring students together to share what they have learned that was new or exciting for them in math today. This is when you and your students work together to evaluate the strategies used and brainstorm alternative strategies.

Seeing patterns (how numbers relate to each other) is basic to math understanding, as is coming up with multiple solutions (more than 1 way to solve a problem). When you encourage your students to share math solutions, you create learners who look for multiple pathways to learning.

This is a great time to create anchor charts on large chart paper to record students' suggestions. Display the charts in your room and add to them as the children's math understandings evolve.

DIFFERENTIATED DAILY LESSON PLAN TEMPLATE

Section 1—Direct Instruction (up to 30 minutes)

Concept (What are you teaching?):

Options (How are you going to present or introduce the concept?):

___ songs   ___ rhymes   ___ graphs
___ calendar activities   ___ whole-group games   ___ related literature
___ teacher modeling   ___ other

Materials needed:

Notes:

Section 2—Exploration & Guided Practice (up to 60 minutes)

Problem(s) (What is the student exploring?):

Guided practice (How is the student reviewing the concept?):

___ task cards   ___ Choice Option Menu   ___ graphic organizers
___ literature connections   ___ graphs   ___ glyphs
___ food activities   ___ interactive Web sites   ___ games
___ math posters   ___ other

Grouping (what grouping options are you using?):

___ small groups   ___ pairs   ___ individuals   ___ multileveled assignments

Materials needed:

Section 3—Sharing (10 to 15 minutes)

Evaluation (Did the strategies work?):

Questions to consider together:
How well did the strategies work?
What are some alternative solutions?
Which strategy did you think worked the best?

Brainstorm:
What did we learn this time?
What can we do differently?

OBSERVATION TO IDENTIFY LEARNING STYLES

Student:_____ Date: _____

   Use this chart to help identify the different learning styles of the students in your classroom. Make multiple copies (1 for each child in your class) and attach the copies to a clipboard or to each child's permanent file folder. Circle the attributes for each child as you observe students in the classroom. Skim through the circles to determine which modality seems to represent the way each child learns best or which one seems to predominate for that child. Complete a chart for each child within the first month of school. You may want to repeat the process after the winter holidays to see if the child has changed.

Visual	Auditory	Kinesthetic
Mind may wander during verbal activities	May talk to self to process material being presented	May touch nearby objects or people
Is a "watcher" rather than a talker	Enjoys talking	Needs to move to process
Likes to organize tasks	Can be distracted by noises or voices	Likes to touch people while working with them
Is a reader	Has trouble with written directions	Moves when studying
Usually is a good speller	Likes to be read to	Enjoys activities
Uses graphics and pictures to remember	Uses steps in a process to remember	Prefers solving problems by doing them
Stays on task easily	Enjoys music	Is a poor speller
Has difficulty with verbal instruction	Will whisper read	Acting things out helps memory
Doodles	Enjoys listening	Talks with gestures
Is usually quiet	Enjoys visiting	Movement helps attention
Prefers to work where it is quiet	Prefers to work with someone else when studying	Needs frequent breaks when studying

Notes:

- Students may exhibit behaviors from more than 1 modality. Those who are equally comfortable with different modalities can be your more flexible learners, because they learn in more than 1 way.

- Students under stress may appear more distractible. It's important to recognize this because some characteristics of students' learning styles may change during the year as children become more comfortable in the classroom or more mature.

- If you plan multiple ways for students to learn, practice, and reflect on their learning, you'll find that all students will feel more relaxed in your classroom and will perform at a higher level.

STUDENT INTEREST INVENTORY

Student:_____ Date: _____

1. In school, this is what I like to do best:_____
_____

2. Outside of school, this is what I like to do best:_____
_____

3. When I grow up I would like to: _____

4. A pet I would like to have is: _____

5. I like to collect: _____

6. My favorite place to be is: _____

7. Something I like to make is: _____

8. My favorite television show is: _____

9. My favorite book is: _____

10. The person in my family I like to spend time with is: _____

11. My favorite thing to do when I am alone is: _____
_____

12. I take lessons outside of school to learn: _____

13. My favorite sport to watch or play is:_____

14. My favorite music is:_____

15. If someone asked me how I felt about school, I would say: ____
_____

16. If someone asked me how I felt about math, I would say: _____
_____

A STUDENT INTERVIEW
TO IDENTIFY MULTIPLE INTELLIGENCES

Student: _____ Date: _____

Ask the student, "What do you like?" Use a 3-point scale to record his answers, with 3 being the most positive (if you're working with a young child, you might want to have him point to a smiley face for "yes," a straight-lipped face for "sometimes," and a frown for "not usually"). Then just skim to see where the highest numbers fall.

Linguistic
Do you like reading and writing? ___
Do you like to be read to? ___
Do you like to talk to people? ___

Logical/mathematical
Do you enjoy working with numbers? ___
Do you enjoy finding patterns? ___
Do you like counting things? ___

Spatial
Do you like drawing and painting? ___
Do you like to build things? ___
Do you like mazes? ___

Bodily/kinesthetic
Do you like to move and act things out? ___
Do you like using manipulatives? ___
Do you like sports or gymnastics? ___

Musical
Do you like to dance? ___
Do you like to sing? ___
Do you enjoy listening to raps, rhymes, and songs? ___

Interpersonal
Do you enjoy being with other people? ___
Do you like to help friends with their problems? ___
Do you like to play games? ___

Intrapersonal
Do you prefer to work alone? ___
Do you think you are a good problem solver? ___
Do you enjoy writing in journals about your feelings? ___

Naturalist
Do you have collections at home of things you've found outside? ___
Do you like to sort things and arrange them? ___
When you go home, do you prefer to be outside? ___

Number Skills Assessment

Assessment is a key part of differentiation. Here's a quick way to assess each child's number skills several times during the year so you can accurately track the growth in the child's skills and understandings.

MATERIALS

- 1 paper copy of the "Individual Number Skills Assessment" reproducible (page 175) for each child
- 1 copy of the "Number Skills" reproducible (pages 176–77) on card stock, enlarged and laminated
- 1 paper copy of the "Class Number Skills Assessment" reproducible (page 178), enlarged

Procedure

Use the "Individual Number Skills Assessment" and the laminated reproducible to assess each student one-on-one. On the chart, record the results for each student in the class. This tells you where in the learning cycle each child needs to begin working on each skill, and it also gives you a better sense of the strengths and weaknesses of the class as a whole.

CLASS NUMBER SKILLS ASSESSMENT

Date _____

Student:	1. Shapes	2. Writes numbers	3. Counts 1s, 2s, 5s, 10s	4. Instant dot recognition	5. One-to-one correspondence	6. Counts backward from	7. Reads numerals to _____	8. Reads number words	9. Plays bean game to _____	10. Flash cards to _____
James	⬭⬭▲◻	All	100/10 20/100	to 6	to 8	from 9	39	six	8	N/A
Sarah	All	All	to 100 /All	to 5	to 10	from 19	all/100	ten	7	N/A
Matthew	0	1–3	1s only to 10	1,2,3 only	to 4	from 5	1 to 5, 10	none	4	N/A

INDIVIDUAL NUMBER SKILLS ASSESSMENT

1. Draws (basic shapes):

2. Writes numbers correctly: 1 2 3 4 5 6 7 8 9 10
Record the numbers the student is able to copy from the laminated reproducible.

3. Rote counts by 1s to _____; 2s to _____; 5s to _____; 10s to _____
Record the highest number the child counts to in the grouping. Suggested quuestions and procedures: "How far do you think you can count?" "Count for me." If the child counts confidently to 100 and stops, ask, "What's after 100?"

4. Instant dot recognition to _____
Test to 6 using the domino patterns on the laminated reproducible.

5. Understands one-to-one correspondence to _____
Test to 10 objects using the laminated reproducible.

6. Counts backward from _____
Instruct the child to "place 8 [or another appropriate number of] beans in a line on the table." Confirm the total, saying, "How many do you have?" Cover 1 bean with a piece of paper and say, "Now how many do you have?" The child should respond without having to recount the beans.

7. Reads numerals to _____
Ask student to read numbers from the Numeral Recognition sections of the laminated reproducible, or use a different sheet with a similar selection of random numbers between 1 and 100.

8. Reads number words: *one, two,* and so on
Ask the student to read the number words on the laminated reproducible.

9. Plays bean game to _____
Have the child count 6 beans into your hand. Put some of the beans in your open hand and keep the rest hidden in your other hand. Ask, "How many beans do I have hidden in this hand?" The child should respond correctly and confidently. Repeat with different quantities. Note: The child should be able to play the bean game with a number of beans that matches her age. Five-year-olds should be able to play all combinations of 5: 2 + 3, 3 + 2, 4 + 1, 1 + 4, 5 + 0, 0 + 5.

10. Basic facts flash cards
Use any set of cards you have to test the instant recognition of facts to 10 (first grade) and facts to 20 (second grade). Be sure to include both addition and subtraction sets. If students are ready, mix the sets.

NUMBER SKILLS

(For use with Individual Number Skills Assessment)

Number Writing

1 2 3 4 5 6 7 8 9 10

Domino Patterns

One-To-One Correspondence

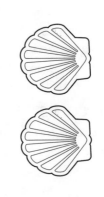 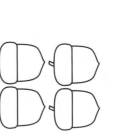 

 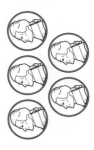 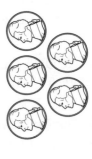        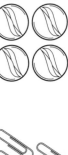

NUMBER SKILLS
(continued)

Numeral Recognition Through 10

3	2	6	4	7	5	9	8	1	10	0

3 2 6 4 7 5 9 8 1 10 0

Numeral Recognition Beyond 10

16 11 46 29 20 19 66 78 12 17

58 100 23 91 73 15 18 13 84 34

Number Words

three nine five one two

four eight six ten seven

CLASS NUMBER SKILLS ASSESSMENT

Date _____

Student:	1. Shapes	2. Writes numbers	3. Counts 1s, 2s, 5s, 10s	4. Instant dot recognition	5. One-to-one correspondence	6. Counts backward from	7. Reads numerals to ___	8. Reads number words	9. Plays bean game to ___	10. Flash cards to ___

REPRODUCIBLE

SUBJECTS FOR MATH PORTFOLIOS

Math portfolios are another ideal way to demonstrate a student's growth over time. The point of a portfolio is to record the progress in each student's mathematical thinking by pulling together representative samples of the child's work (selected jointly by you and the student). Use portfolios to further encourage student reflection and to integrate your curriculum. And use them again to show parents, fellow teachers, and administrators what your students have learned.

What's appropriate for inclusion in a student's portfolio? Here are some topic headings to get you started. Just copy the labels below, cut them apart, and staple them to pages of student portfolios.

Student Labels for Portfolio Pages

An Answer to an Open-Ended Math Question (Date:_____)
An Individual Math Project (Date:_____)
Story Problems I Have Made Up (Date:_____)
Drawings Done for Math (Date:_____)
Wonderings About Possible Solutions (Date:_____)
Math Poster Design (Date:_____)
Outside Work or Investigations Done for Math (Date:_____)
Graphs Done for a Literary or Other Subject Area Project (Date:_____)
Work I Have Corrected That Shows My Growth in Thinking (Date:_____)

Teacher Labels for Portfolio Pages

A Description with a Photo of a Group Project (Date:_____)
A Math-Related Science or Social Studies Project (Date:_____)
Story Problems That Are Student-Generated (Date:_____)
Papers the Student Has Self-Corrected (Date:_____)
Photos of Group Graphs (Date:_____)
Teacher Anecdotes (Date:_____)
Rubric for a Project or Investigation (Date:_____)
Completed Menu or Agenda (Date:_____)
Teacher Observations of Growth in Independence (Date:_____)

Ideas for Math Journals

Math journals are a wonderful tool for differentiation. Maintaining a math journal encourages student reflection and allows students to build on their strengths. Journals allow students to process their learning in many different ways and to demonstrate their learning through a variety of products. Journals also give you an excellent means of assessing progress of individual students over time—and of documenting that progress for students and their parents. These are just a few of the things you might ask students to include in their journals.

- An answer to an open-ended math question
- A description of a group project, with a photo
- An individual math project
- A math-related science or social studies project
- Graphs done for a project in some other subject area
- Word problems that are student generated
- Drawings done for math
- Outside work or investigations done for math
- Math poster design
- Wonderings about possible solutions
- Teacher responses

Mini Math Lab Books

Sometimes you'll want students to use their math journals as permanent records, to show how their thinking evolves over the course of the year. Other times, students will need a place to record their thinking just for the day or just while they're involved in a particular activity. That's where mini math lab books come in. These 3 formats will give your students a variety of small books to use in their math investigations. The students can create them as needed or you can enlist parent volunteers to make them up ahead of time.

Stagger Book

1. Start with 2 sheets of 8 1/2 x 11-inch paper, positioned vertically.

2. Place Sheet A on top of Sheet B so that the upper edge of Sheet A is staggered approximately 1 inch above the upper edge of Sheet B.

3. Turn over the top edges of both sheets so that each of the staggered edges is approximately 1 inch from the one above it.

4. Crease along the fold.

5. Staple along the fold to hold the pages in place.

6. To use the book, position it so the staples are at the top edge and the pages get progressively longer.

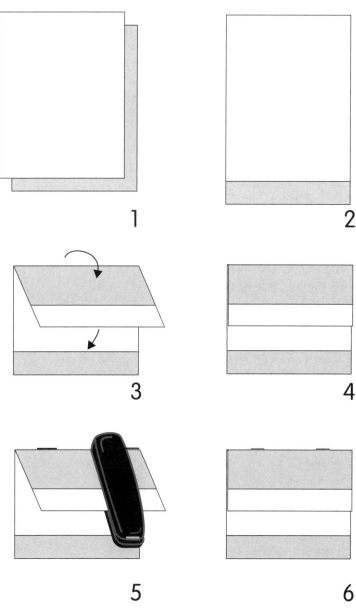

Variations

1. Instead of stapling, punch 2 holes near the fold and hold together with yarn or string.

2. Start with 3 pages to get a 6-page book or start with 4 pages to get an 8-page book—you've incorporated another math lesson at the same time!

Poof Book

1. Start with an 8 1/2 x 11-inch sheet of paper positioned vertically. Fold the paper in half horizontally.

2. Repeat.

3. Take the folded paper and fold the whole thing in half once more—but this time the fold should be vertical. You've now folded the paper into eighths.

4. Open the sheet half way (to 8 1/2 x 5 1/2 inches) and turn it so the fold is at the bottom.

5. Cut along the vertical fold line from the folded edge. Stop when you reach the horizontal fold line.

6. Open the paper completely.

7. Fold it in half lengthwise.

8. Turn the paper 90 degrees, grasp the outer edges, and push them together.

9. Crease all folds again to form a book.

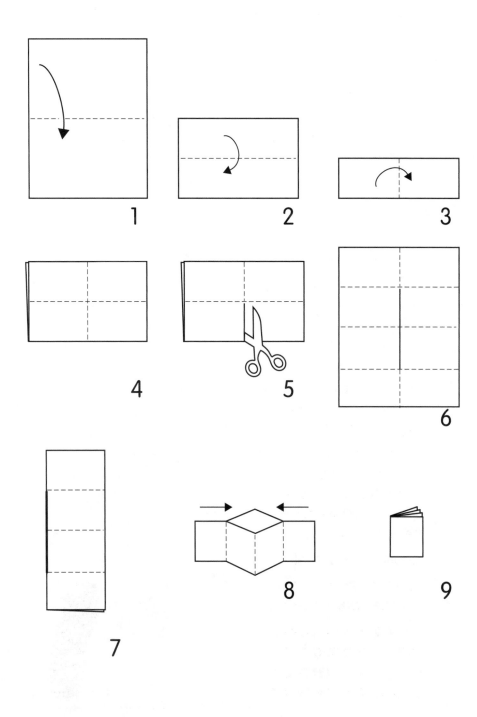

Slit Book

1. You'll need two 8 1/2 x 11-inch sheets of paper. Take the first sheet and fold it in half along the 8 1/2-inch side.

2. About an inch from each end, make a small vertical snip on the fold. These snips are your markers.

3. Make a shallow cut between the 2 snips, cutting off the folded edge.

4. Take the second sheet of paper and fold it just like the first one.

5. Once again make a pair of small vertical snips about an inch from each end.

6. On this sheet, cut in along the fold from each end to the snip.

7. Roll up the second sheet along the 11-inch side and insert it into the hole in the first sheet.

8. Release the rolled-up sheet and adjust it to form a 4-page response book.

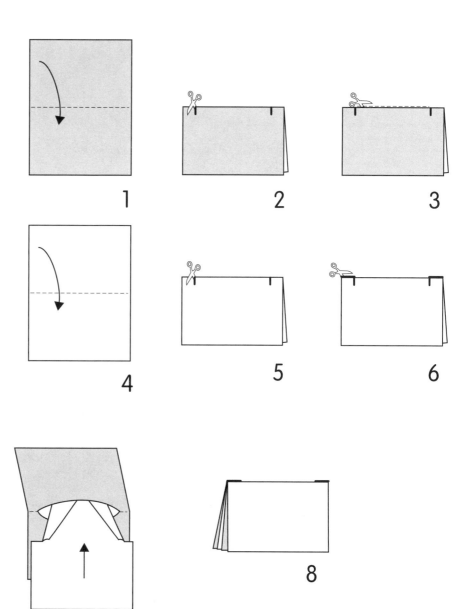

RESOURCES

PRINT RESOURCES

Baker, Johnny and Ann. 1991. *Raps and rhymes in maths*. Portsmouth, NH: Heinemann.

Burns, Marilyn. 1992. *About teaching mathematics: a K–8 resource.* Portsmouth, NH: Heinemann.

Guzzetta, Torrie, and Pat Gilbert. 2005. *Glyphs & math: how to collect, interpret, and analyze data.* Peterborough, NH: Crystal Springs Books.

Lilburn, Pat, and Pam Rawson. 1994. *Let's talk math: encouraging children to explore ideas.* Portsmouth, NH: Heinemann.

National Council of Teachers of Mathematics. 1989. *Curriculum and evaluation standards for school mathematics.* Reston, VA: National Council of Teachers of Mathematics.

Newman, Vicki. 1994. *Math journals: tools for authentic assessment.* San Leonardo, CA: Teaching Resource Center.

Rowan, Thomas, and Barbara Bourne. 1994. *Thinking like mathematicians: putting the K–4 NCTM standards into practice.* Portsmouth, NH: Heinemann.

Satariano, Patricia. 1994. *Storytime math time: math explorations in children's literature.* Palo Alto, CA: Dale Seymour.

Schiller, Pam Byrne, and Lynne Peterson. 1997. *Count on math: activities for small hands and lively minds.* Beltsville, MD: Gryphon House.

Smutny, Joan Franklin, and S. E. von Fremd. 2004. *Differentiating for the young child: teaching strategies across the content areas (K–3).* Thousand Oaks, CA: Corwin Press.

Welchman-Tischler, Rosamond. 1992. *How to use children's literature to teach mathematics.* Reston, VA: National Council of Teachers of Mathematics.

Whitin, David J., and Sandra Wilde. 1992. *Read any good math lately?* Portsmouth, NH: Heinemann.

-----. 1995. *It's the story that counts: more children's books for mathematical learning.* Portsmouth, NH: Heinemann.

MATHEMATICS FROM THE INTERNET

www.aimsedu.org
   Activities for math and science integration are available for purchase and download.

www.connieseducation.com
   A source of many unusual dice.

http://countdown.luc.edu/

This site has many ideas for you as well as your students. It contains short video clips, each with a teacher explaining a concept and working with a student.

www.creativemathematics.com

Kim Sutton's Web site is a rich source of classroom material and has a downloadable list of student trade books related to math topics—all available for purchase and download.

http://www.doe.state.in.us/exceptional/gt/tiered_curriculum/welcome.html

This site contains tiered lesson plans for math, science, and language arts at different grade levels (K–12). Lessons are tiered by readiness, interest, and learning style.

http://illuminations.nctm.org

A great site from the National Council of Teachers of Mathematics. Select from "Activities," "Lessons," and "Standards."

www.k111.k12.il.us/king/math.htm

The site features several links to interactive math sites by topic.

www.kidzone.ws/math

This Web site has games and downloadable work sheets as well as online games for practicing basic facts.

www.marcopolo-education.org

Click on "Teacher Resources" and then "Lesson Plan Index" to link to many sites that use math at different grade levels.

http://math.rice.edu/~lanius/

This site has great games and activities for all levels of learners.

www.matti.usu.edu/nlvm/nav/vlibrary.html

Younger and older students will enjoy the activities here, which are tied to NCTM standards.

www.nwrel.org/assessment/lessonplans.php?

Click on "Reading" and you will get to "Reading—Lesson Plans." It includes many ideas for integrating math and literature.

www.orientaltrading.com

A source of playing cards in several sizes, dice, and many small novelty items for sorting and classifying.

www.pbskids.org/cyberchase/games

The site includes codes, patterns, and analytical thinking for middle and upper grades.

INDEX

Note: Page numbers in *italics* indicate reproducibles.